Praise

'No one is born a crisis _____ _____ive formal training on how to bec_ __ _ne. That's why this book is so important: it gives busy executives the knowledge and confidence to protect business reputation on the worst days of their business lives.'
> – **Anik Michaud**, Group Director Corporate Relations, Anglo American

'In an ever riskier world, the requirement to plan for crisis has never been greater. If you're unsure where to start, I can think of no better place than this book.'
> – **Steve Parkinson**, Former Group Head of Operational Resilience, Sky

'Doing and saying the right things under the intense pressure of a crisis is a unique challenge. Through this book, Jonathan Hemus reveals the secrets of protecting business reputation under fire.'
> – **Aoife Clarke**, Head of Communications & Marketing, Lidl Ireland & Northern Ireland

'Anyone aspiring to lead crisis management within their organisation should read this book. *Crisis Proof* equips them with the principles, framework and practical tips to protect their organisations from harm and plays a vital part in developing the crisis managers of the future.'

> – **Professor Pavel Albores**, Director, Aston University CRISIS Centre

'Jonathan Hemus has distilled his twenty-five years' crisis management experience into a book which is essential reading for anyone wanting to prepare their business to respond effectively to a crisis. Read it now (before it's too late!).'

> – **Paul Newman**, Former VP Communications, Procter & Gamble and eBay

'As one of the foremost experts in crisis management, Jonathan Hemus is exceptionally well qualified to write this book. Act on what he says and you won't go far wrong.'

> – **Dennis Flynn**, OBE, Founder and former Managing Director, Crisis Solutions

'There are many books on how to respond to a crisis but few that equip you to effectively prepare for them. *Crisis Proof* tells you everything you need to know about how to create and maintain an effective crisis management programme.'

> – **Claire Gosnell**, Global Head of Brand, Communications and Marketing, Clifford Chance LLP

CRISIS PROOF

How to prepare for the worst day of your business life

JONATHAN HEMUS

R^ethink

First published in Great Britain in 2020
by Rethink Press (www.rethinkpress.com)

© Copyright Jonathan Hemus

Cover image © Shutterstock | Jag_cz

Contents

Foreword   1

Introduction   5
   Foundations   10
   Assess   11
   Plan   12
   Train   13
   Exercise   14
   Response   14
   What this book will enable you to do   15

SECTION ONE Foundations   17

1 The Impact Of Crisis And How To Avoid It   19
   The impact of crisis   20
   Fatal flaws   22
   Why even smart companies get it wrong   25
   Summary   32
   Questions   32

2   **How To Create A Robust Crisis Management
    Framework**   **35**

What is crisis management?   38

How does crisis management fit with
interrelated areas?   40

The four essential pillars of crisis
preparedness   45

Summary   47

Questions   48

3   **Beginning Your Crisis Management
    Programme**   **51**

Taking stock   52

Forming your crisis management taskforce   54

Summary   64

Questions   65

4   **How To Secure Executive Buy-In**   **67**

Demonstrate the cost of failure   69

Make it personal   70

Communicate the broader benefits   72

Get your timing right   73

Build alliances with like-minded colleagues   76

Start small and grow   76

Deploy trusted third parties   77

Get your own house in order first   78

Summary   79

Questions   80

SECTION TWO Assess   **81**

5 Crisis Culture   **83**

Recognising a crisis-prone culture   84

Summary   93

Questions   94

6 How To Assess Your Risk Landscape   **95**

Why understanding your risk landscape is
important   96

Building a picture of your risk landscape   97

Identifying reputational risk   99

Identifying killer risks   101

Summary   102

Questions   103

SECTION THREE Plan   **105**

**7 How Scenario Planning Can Build Crisis
Resilience**   **107**

What is scenario planning?   108

What are the benefits of scenario planning?   110

How to run a scenario planning session   111

Summary   116

Questions   117

8 How To Develop Your Crisis Management Plan   **119**

The purpose of a crisis management plan   120

How to develop a plan that works under
pressure   123

Essential content 125

Summary 131

Questions 131

9 How To Develop Your Crisis Communication
Plan 133

The role of communication in crisis
management 134

The purpose of a crisis communication plan 137

Essential content 138

Summary 144

Questions 145

SECTION FOUR Train 147

10 Creating An Effective Crisis Management Team 149

The role of your crisis management team 151

Core roles 152

Specialist roles and experts 163

Your extended crisis management team 165

Summary 166

Questions 167

11 How To Develop A Highly Effective Crisis
Management Team 169

How to brief your crisis management team 170

How to train your crisis management team 173

Summary 177

Questions 178

SECTION FIVE Exercise   **179**

12 Why Exercise?   **181**

The purpose of exercising   182

Different exercise types and the benefits of
each   187

Summary   194

Questions   194

13 How To Ensure Successful Exercise Delivery   **197**

Planning   199

Delivery   206

Summary   212

Questions   212

SECTION SIX Response   **213**

14 Fundamentals Of A Successful Crisis Response   **215**

Summary   222

Questions   222

15 How To Continuously Improve   **223**

Crisis management policy   224

Learning from exercises   225

Learning from live incidents   228

Summary   233

Questions   234

16 Concluding Thoughts   235

  References   237

Acknowledgements   255

The Author   257

Foreword

I have never wanted a job as much as I wanted to be Head of Group Business Resilience for Cathay Pacific Airways. I had been part of the response teams at other airlines for multiple fatal aircraft accidents and the 9/11 terrorist attacks, but mostly from a crisis communications perspective.

This was a chance to influence how a well-respected organisation planned to respond at all levels on a global scale to whatever crisis befell it, to ensure a humanitarian focus was front and centre at every turn, and to help talented people become extraordinary at duties they never envisaged having to undertake.

I was invited up to the executive floor to be told I had been successful in my quest. As composed as I wanted to be, I know a small smile sneaked out. I rushed home to share the news with my family and we celebrated a relished career victory.

I could not sleep the first night after taking up the role. I lay in bed thinking about every aircraft we had flying around the world at that very moment. I thought of all my colleagues at work in facilities everywhere from Johannesburg to Kathmandu. I suddenly found myself worried about things I had never worried about before... the weather, potential security breaches, data integrity, even fire extinguishers and more.

I sat up in unfamiliar panic wondering just what the hell I had done.

That night, I would have loved to have had a copy of this book. After reading some of Jonathan's sage advice, I might even have fallen back to sleep. As it was, I have now spent many years learning first-hand how to establish, manage and maintain a proper crisis management programme. Fortunately, you can skip the sleepless nights by spending some quality time with Jonathan's experience and counsel, all thoughtfully sequenced for you in the following pages.

Although I believe any crisis manager would find Jonathan's book a useful refresher, it is really meant for those of you who have had crisis management duties thrust upon you. If that's the case for you, I sympathise. If you do not relish the role as I do, I can only imagine how much more daunting the responsibilities may seem.

This book can make the transition less stressful. From sharing fundamentals to providing practical insight,

Jonathan brings together a wealth of knowledge and experience in a concise, easy-to-read and easily understood format. This is material you can instantly put to use in your organisation, meaning you can immediately start making an impact.

The solid advice contained herein comes from someone who has not only walked the talk, but truly cares about helping people and organisations succeed. Jonathan was finishing this book at the height of the initial COVID-19 crisis in between people actively seeking his counsel. I remember during a late-night phone conversation we had during this time that his primary concern remained helping individuals, whether they were paying clients or not, weather an unfathomable storm. That is dedication to one's craft.

I love crisis management. I live for it. That may not be the case for you. But if you have been handed this assignment, the lives of your colleagues and the stability of your organisation may someday rest on what you have done since taking over the role.

Do yourself a favour. Read this book. Learn from it. Take a giant step forward in ensuring peace of mind for everyone who is depending on you.

Gus Whitcomb
Head of Group Business Resilience, Cathay Pacific Airways Ltd, Hong Kong SAR

Introduction

'By the time you hear the thunder, it's too late to build the ark.'
— Unknown

I didn't set out to be a crisis management consultant – who does? With an interest in business, communication and people, a career in public relations seemed to be the perfect choice when I graduated from the University of Liverpool. Consequently, the formative years of my career were spent editing the company newsletter, drafting press releases and investor relations for a then FTSE 100 business, Delta PLC.

A move into PR consultancy created the opportunity to work closely with the CEO of a rapidly growing business as he planned acquisitions, courted the national business media, briefed institutional investors and dealt with major business challenges. Spending so much time learning from an experienced and dynamic business leader at such an early stage of my career was a privilege. It sealed my fascination with business and businesspeople.

As I became more and more engrossed in the world of business, I was inspired by leaders who, when confronted with a potentially catastrophic event, stepped forward to protect not only their own interests but also those of their stakeholders.

My earliest memory of such a leader is Michael Bishop (now Baron Glendonbrook), chief executive of the airline British Midland, who led its response to a major air crash in 1989. His speed of response, presence at the scene of the accident, personal concern for the victims, pitch-perfect media interviews and the confidence he provided to colleagues through his words and deeds were critical elements in British Midland's recovery from the tragic accident.

It was his leadership, humanity and courage to do and say the right things under enormous pressure that first made me consider a career in crisis management and ultimately led me to become global head of crisis management at Porter Novelli in 1999.

As my interest in crisis management developed, I also observed 'anti-heroes', business leaders who were unable to rise to the challenge when crisis struck. I was puzzled as to how these experienced business leaders could fail so spectacularly while others succeeded.

It still saddens me to see admired, successful businesses destroy themselves as a result of poor crisis management. It angers me even more to witness the unnecessary harm wreaked upon employees, customers, local communities and investors as a result.

Crises don't destroy businesses. It is the organisation's response to the crisis which does that. My passion is to give business leaders the capability and confidence to succeed, whatever the world throws at them.

In this book I will share my knowledge, experience and insights to ensure that, when crisis strikes, your business can protect not just itself but also the lives and livelihoods of its stakeholders. Mishandled crises cause needless devastation, but it doesn't have to be that way. I want all business leaders to have the culture, capability and confidence to prevent or overcome crises so they avoid harm to lives, jobs, communities, reputation and financial value.

This book is aimed at businesses who share this vision, the kind of businesses that embrace crisis management planning not because a regulator has told them they must, but because they sincerely believe it is the right thing to do. They are driven by both a sense of responsibility to their stakeholders *and* self-interest.

Leaders of successful, growing and admired businesses arc mindful of the risks they face and concerned that a crisis could seriously harm their business, reputation and stakeholders. They have a genuine desire to protect their business in the event of crisis but are fearful they currently lack the wherewithal to do so. They worry that, if a crisis strikes, the consequences for their business and its stakeholders could be devastating.

By applying the approach outlined in this book, this fear can be replaced with confidence, reassurance and peace of mind, knowing they are geared up to do and say the right things on the worst days of their careers.

Few businesses employ a full-time head of crisis management responsible for preparing their firm for their worst nightmare (and if you do have this job, your experience and knowledge mean you probably don't need to read this book). Instead, accountability for this most critical of tasks usually lands with smart, successful yet busy executives whose main role is heading up another function such as corporate communications, legal or HR.

Few of these people have deep knowledge of crisis management. Why would they? They've built a successful career in their chosen profession and with a full workload in their 'day job' there's little time to become crisis management experts too. Yet they are given the additional responsibility for ensuring their business and its employees do and say the right things under extreme pressure when crisis strikes.

Why? Because they are respected and valued by their senior management colleagues for their professional expertise and personal qualities. They can be trusted to get this important job done.

This book is written for them. It is designed to give savvy, successful but time-poor executives the knowledge, insights and framework to successfully lead a programme of crisis management planning, training and exercising – the kind of programme that will ensure their business does the right thing when crisis strikes to not only protect business reputation, but also the lives and livelihoods of all those affected by an incident.

There are books that outline principles for crisis management or how you should respond to a crisis event. This isn't one of them (though in Chapter 14 I do set out some of my insider tips for crisis response based on twenty-five years' experience).

It is my firm belief that successful crisis management is much more about what you do before the crisis than after it. Combining the right corporate mindset with a commitment to crisis management planning, training and exercising all but guarantees you will respond to a crisis in the right way.

So, this book focuses on what you must do to make your business crisis ready. It covers the following main areas.

Foundations

The impact of crisis and why smart companies get it wrong

The fact you are reading this book suggests you need little convincing of the need for crisis management. But for avoidance of doubt (and to help convince any sceptics in your management team) this chapter outlines the many impacts of a crisis and how to inoculate yourself from them.

How to create a robust crisis management framework

Understanding the purpose of crisis management and how it differs from related disciplines such as business continuity, emergency response and risk management is the essential first step to protecting your business. Without this you may think you have a comprehensive crisis management plan in place, when in fact it is nothing of the kind. This chapter sets the record straight, explains how to assess existing materials and provides a summary of the constituent elements of a robust crisis management framework.

Beginning your crisis preparedness programme

Crisis management is a team sport and you cannot create a crisis-resilient organisation on your own, no matter how hard you try. This chapter explains how to resource your crisis management planning, training and exercising programme with colleagues and specialist partners.

How to secure executive buy-in

Truly effective crisis management requires the commitment, engagement and support of your leadership team and, in particular, your CEO. This chapter outlines how to secure their active involvement on your crisis management journey.

Assess

The importance of a crisis-resistant culture

Planning, training and exercising are all essential if you want to avoid the consequences of a crisis but without the right culture, they cannot be relied upon to prevent a mishandled crisis. This chapter outlines the characteristics of crisis-prone and crisis-resilient cultures, how to recognise them in your business and instil behaviours, values and attitudes to underpin crisis resilience.

How to assess your risk landscape

Crisis management planning begins with understanding your vulnerabilities. This chapter explains how to identify and prioritise your risk landscape. Crucially, it reveals how to uncover the killer risks that could bring your business to its knees.

Plan

How scenario planning can build crisis resilience

Knowing what your risks are is the starting point for managing them. Understanding how they might play out and how best to respond to them is the role of scenario planning. This chapter explains how to scenario plan against your critical risks.

How to develop your crisis management plan

A good crisis management plan provides the framework for a successful crisis response. This chapter sets out the purpose of your crisis management plan, its structure, essential content and common traps to avoid.

How to develop your crisis communication plan

Successfully managing a crisis requires a business to do two things: fix the problem and communicate effectively with affected stakeholders. As many businesses have found to their cost, a crisis communication plan is not the same as a crisis management plan. This chapter outlines the role of your crisis communication plan, what it should contain and recommendations on how to prepare for stakeholder communication.

Train

Creating your crisis management team

Understanding who would need to be involved in your crisis response is essential if you are to hit the ground running when a crisis explodes. This chapter explains the roles required on your team plus the characteristics, skills and qualities demanded by each role to help you select those best equipped to fulfil them. It also looks at the specialists and advisors you may need to supplement your team with expert input.

How to develop a highly effective crisis management team

Assigning roles on the crisis management team is just the first step. To be effective under the intense pressure of a crisis they must know how your crisis management plan works and what will be expected of them in their role. This chapter explains how to brief and train your crisis management team members.

Exercise

Why exercise?

Exercising should lie at the heart of your crisis preparedness programme. This chapter explains why and reveals benefits of exercising that go beyond crisis management. It also sets out your options in terms of exercise format, the purpose, pros and cons of each.

How to ensure successful exercise delivery

Being responsible for the successful delivery of a crisis management simulation is a heavy burden. Exposing senior management to a pressurised situation carries obvious risks. This chapter provides a template for designing and delivering exercises that build both crisis resilience and the support of your colleagues.

Response

Fundamentals of a successful crisis response

This book focuses on how to prepare for a crisis through planning, training and exercising. However, this chapter highlights some of the critical principles for a successful response. They are based on my years of experience observing and advising crisis management teams and include the most common mistakes plus the fundamentals teams must get right if they are to prevail in a crisis. They serve as an *aide mémoire* to ensure your crisis management team remains on track if crisis hits.

How to continuously improve

Advance planning and preparation underpin an effective crisis response, but what you do after an incident also plays an important part in your crisis resilience. This chapter explains how to learn from your own experiences, and those of others, to make you even better prepared to deal with a crisis.

What this book will enable you to do

This book is not designed to turn you into a full-time crisis manager: you already have a full-time job about which you are passionate and have built up significant expertise and experience.

However, accountability for making your business crisis ready is a big responsibility. When the worst happens, all eyes will be on you as the planning, training and exercising you have put in place are put to the test.

This book's role is to fill in critical gaps in your knowledge of crisis preparedness. Its aim is to be practical, not theoretical, and to bring to your attention the things that really matter when preparing a business for crisis.

Crisis Proof provides an informed framework, insights and insider knowledge to enable you to be the crisis management champion for your company. It gives you a clear understanding of what is required for your company to be ready for a crisis. It clarifies the purpose of crisis management plans and what must be included in them. It reveals the characteristics of a successful crisis exercise so you can ensure they are present when you specify a simulation.

Ultimately, by following the guidance contained in this book, you will be able to sleep peacefully at night knowing you have instilled in your organisation the capability and confidence to protect its business and reputation, whatever the world may throw at it.

SECTION ONE
FOUNDATIONS

ONE

The Impact Of Crisis And How To Avoid It

'It takes twenty years to build a reputation and five minutes to lose it. If you think about that you'll do things differently.'
— Warren Buffett, Berkshire Hathaway

I f a crisis strikes your business, you risk losing everything you've ever worked for: reputation, revenue, respect, value and trust.

In an uncertain and risky world, the likelihood of a crisis hitting your business is higher than ever before. Greater transparency through social media and diminished trust in business mean that reputational damage can be quick and severe if you are unprepared to do and say the right things under pressure.

Protecting the value in your business means being ready to respond quickly, confidently and effectively to an escalating situation. Completing the crisis management planning, training and exercising programme outlined in this book means you will be ready to do so.

The impact of crisis

After Boeing grounded its 737 MAX aircraft in March 2019 following two crashes in which 346 people lost their lives, its CEO Dennis Muilenburg was forced to stand down and the company announced its first annual loss in more than two decades. It also revealed the cost of handling the crisis was expected to be $18.6 billion, over twice its original estimate.

When UK bank TSB mishandled an IT upgrade in April 2018, leaving customers without service for weeks, it spent £125 million on customer compensation, £49 million in relation to fraud and operational losses, £122 million on technical fixes, and £34 million on waived fees and charges. That's £330 million directly attributable to putting the problem right. They also made a £105.4 million loss in 2018 compared to a profit the year before. More than 80,000 customers switched to competitors, with the peak customer loss occurring in Q2, immediately after the fiasco. CEO Paul Pester left the business.

Corporate history is littered with examples of businesses who lost significant value as a result of crises.

Others such as Arthur Andersen, PanAm and Thomas Cook simply ceased to exist due, at least in part, to their mishandling of a crisis.

Crisis management is a high-stakes game, but it's not just about the money. Mishandled crises wreak havoc on the lives and livelihoods of those affected by them. Employees may lose their jobs. Communities may lose investment, homes or even lives. Customers may be without a service or product they rely upon in their daily lives. Suppliers may go out of business as the company at the heart of the crisis cuts back production. Investors lose money.

It doesn't have to be this way. With the right culture and leadership plus a commitment to planning, training and exercising, businesses can prevent crises from occurring or respond so well that their stakeholders, reputation and value are protected.

As Gus Whitcomb, head of crisis management at Cathay Pacific, said:

> 'I once had a CEO who really frustrated me. He used to say, "We're at our best when things are at their worst." That was such a self-defeating prophecy because if your company committed a quarter of the resources it takes to fight the fire when it's already raging to preventing that same fire from igniting at the beginning, we wouldn't even be doing this.'

Indeed, statistical evidence from the consultancy Oxford Metrica shows that crises can be an opportunity to *increase* value if business leaders prove themselves capable of passing what they call 'the acid test of management'.

What is certainly true is that a crisis is a pivotal moment for a business. Manage it well and you will be rewarded with increased stakeholder trust. Fail to meet expectations and the damage can be catastrophic.

Fatal flaws

When I observe organisations struggling to effectively manage a crisis, a number of characteristics are usually displayed.

Firstly, they seem too slow to respond, taking hours (or more) to do or say anything of substance. However, the pace of response demanded in a crisis is quicker than ever before.

Bad news spreads at lightning speed. Research conducted by the law firm Freshfields Bruckhaus Deringer found that 28% of crises spread internationally within an hour and 69% of them spread internationally within twenty-four hours. Unfortunately, it took an average of twenty-one hours for the organisations at the heart of those crises to respond to them.

Reputation, trust and relationships are all at stake and what you do in the first hours of an incident has a disproportionate influence on your ultimate fate.

This was illustrated in a 2016 *Financial Times* article, which compared the time taken to respond to a crisis with the impact on share price.

It revealed that Volkswagen took 476 days from receipt of internal emails questioning emission test results in 2014 before admitting that there was a problem and suffered a share price fall of 45%. In the same year, General Motors took just thirteen days between their new CEO being informed of the issue and announcing the recall of thousands of cars on safety grounds and experienced a share price fall of only 6%.

The same pattern was observed in the pharmaceutical sector. Merck took 1,065 days before recalling its Vioxx pain drug in 2004 and suffered a share price hit of 46%, while Johnson and Johnson decided to recall Tylenol five days after a poisoning scare in 1982 and limited the share price damage to 9.5%.

A slow initial response is often followed by a reactive approach to unfolding events, without ever getting ahead of the situation.

This was true of Whirlpool's response to discovering a fire safety issue with some of its tumble dryer models.

It initiated a product recall of the affected dryers in July 2019, three and a half years after first admitting there was a problem.

Despite knowing the fire risk, Whirlpool continued to advise customers to use their machines. Only after pressure from consumer group Which? and the UK's Trading Standards did Whirlpool recall the products and tell customers not to use their machines until they had been modified or replaced.

Whirlpool had the opportunity to get ahead of this crisis but failed to take advantage of it. If it had issued a full product recall immediately upon becoming aware of the issue, consumers and the media would have recognised its efforts to protect people's safety, even if that meant incurring a short-term financial cost. Instead, Whirlpool failed to seize this opportunity and jeopardised the trust of its stakeholders in the process.

Inappropriate communication or clumsy language can cause organisations to appear uncaring and cold. In 2017, when videos of a passenger being dragged off a United Airlines flight after refusing to give up his seat went viral, the airline issued a statement apologising only for the need to 're-accommodate' customers on that flight, not for causing harm to one of its passengers. The company's use of corporate, cold language to respond to an emotive human situation made its position worse rather than better.

Even when messages are well conceived, sometimes logistical flaws mean that organisations fail to communicate them effectively. All too frequently, call centres are overwhelmed (or lack the information they need), social media channels are silent and websites continue to present the usual corporate story with no information about the raging crisis. On occasions, under the weight of traffic, the website simply crashes.

Perhaps most damaging of all is when an organisation adds fuel to the fire with a confused or contradictory response. Sometimes head office communicates a different message from its in-country team. On other occasions senior management state one thing while frontline staff say another. Crises thrive on conflict and nothing is more damaging to an organisation than internal conflict.

Why even smart companies get it wrong

What causes experienced executives in successful businesses to respond inappropriately to a crisis?

In some cases, the reasons are strategic and profound, stemming from inadequacies in culture. Maybe the organisation communicates too slowly because of its hierarchy, requiring two or three levels of approval before anything can be said. Or it has a risk-averse culture, which prevents decisions being made quickly in the event of a crisis.

Leadership is another critical factor. Not every chief executive is prepared to act and speak quickly in the event of something going wrong.

This is certainly true of foreign exchange company Travelex, which was hit by a cyber-attack on 31 December 2019. The attack brought down its entire operations and company-critical systems were out of action for weeks. The ramifications were far-reaching. Employees around the world were forced to resort to pen and paper and Travelex's banking partners were unable to conduct foreign exchange transactions.

Despite the widespread impact of the attack, Travelex delayed its communication response. It took two days to communicate that its services were offline. Furthermore, it was a full seventeen days before Travelex's CEO Tony D'Souza commented publicly on the issue.

The absence of communication made an already complex situation even more challenging to overcome. In the absence of information from the company, news reporters sought comment from disgruntled customers and frustrated employees. Had Travelex instead communicated quickly, transparently and regularly, they would have been able to influence the narrative and reduce reputational impact.

Overbearing legal influence can also cause organisations to respond too slowly or inappropriately. Legal advisors are a critical part of any crisis response team, but an overly legalistic response can result in a communication approach and speed that are not in an organisation's best long-term interests.

This was the dilemma travel company Thomas Cook faced in the aftermath of an incident in which two children died from carbon monoxide poisoning while on a Thomas Cook holiday in 2006. Due to the legal implications of the case, the company resisted apologising to the children's parents for fear of being found criminally liable.

In November 2014, the then CEO of Thomas Cook Peter Fankhauser told the inquest into the children's deaths: 'I feel so thoroughly, from the deepest of my heart, sorry but there's no need to apologise because there was no wrongdoing by Thomas Cook.' Finally, in May 2015 – nine years after the incident – Thomas Cook did apologise in a letter sent to the children's parents.

No amount of legal advice can justify behaviour like this. It is not only uncaring and hurtful to the victims of the crisis, but also contrary to the best interests of the business.

As Steven Stewart, director of communications at public transport company Stagecoach says: 'Legal advice should not stop you doing what you know is the "right thing". If you take decisions which are for the long-term benefit of both the business and your reputation, the organisation is much more likely to survive and prosper.'

There are no quick fixes to these deep-seated issues, though they can be addressed over time (a topic I will explore in more detail in Chapter 5, which is about crisis culture).

More often, a suboptimal response to a crisis occurs not as a result of culture or structure, but simply because of the unique characteristics of a crisis.

In my experience, organisations dealing with a crisis for the first time (especially without a crisis management plan, training or exercising) will experience a number of the following challenges.

- **Fear, pressure and uncertainty impede their ability to operate effectively:** these factors combine to cause severe stress resulting in an instinctive 'fight, flight or freeze' response, which is rarely the best antidote to a crisis.

- **Normal ways of working fail to get the job done:** a crisis is *not* business as usual – it is quite literally an extraordinary event. Consequently, a swifter, more focused and directive approach to leadership, communication and management is required to seize control and exert influence.

- **People leap to action without thinking:** when a crisis erupts, the natural instinct is to want to fix it. But acting without thinking can make a bad situation even worse if your actions are ill-considered.

- **People prioritise the wrong things and forget others:** there's always too much to do in a crisis and never enough time. Without a plan, it's unlikely you will remember and prioritise the most important things you need to do.

- **The 'fog of war' leads to confusion and mistakes are made:** crises are characterised by a lack of facts but a mass of rumour, half-truths and unconfirmed information, especially in the early stages. Decision-making and communication based on incomplete and inaccurate information are bound to be flawed.

- **Lack of people, tools and resources:** a crisis places an extreme burden on an organisation's resources, way beyond those required on a normal day. Unless you can draw upon a significantly increased resource pool during a crisis, you are unlikely to prevail.

All the above challenges are completely understandable: crises are by their very nature unusual, pressurised and uncertain. As a consequence, adrenaline flows through our bodies and the ability for rational thought diminishes.

Overcoming a purely instinctive reaction is critical if you are to exert a positive influence over the situation with which you are faced. Your crisis management plan provides the framework for doing this.

This was well illustrated by the response of theme park operator Merlin when teenage riders with life-changing injuries were trapped for hours on its Smiler roller-coaster ride, following a crash at Alton Towers Park in 2015.

Its response was exemplary and played a major role in protecting its reputation and value. The nature and speed of its words and actions indicate clearly that it was based upon a well-conceived and rehearsed crisis management plan.

How do we know that? The speed of its communication response, for one. Its normal Alton Towers website was taken down within minutes and replaced with a more sober holding page detailing news of unfolding events. For Merlin to make this change so quickly demonstrates forethought and planning.

This contrasts with other businesses, which have allowed their normal websites to remain visible, sometimes with upbeat or promotional content, which clashes with the seriousness of the crisis they are facing. An example of this was the death of thirty-four Lonmin mine workers during protests at its Marikana mine in South Africa in 2012. Despite the tragic events,

Lonmin's corporate website still featured images of happy, smiling miners on its homepage, waving cheerily at the camera.

Merlin's social media response was also well judged. Within minutes of the accident the company's social media team was communicating about it via its Facebook page and Twitter feed.

Not only did it post regular updates, but it also responded individually to questions from members of the public and other stakeholders. That level of interactivity could not have happened without planning and the empowerment of its social media team.

Engagement with the traditional media was equally impressive. Rather than hide behind his lawyers, Nick Varney, Merlin's chief executive, was quick to visit the scene and began communicating with the media on site. His words were well judged, focusing on care for those affected, taking responsibility for what had happened and a commitment to put it right, saying from the outset: 'I would like to express my sincerest regret and apology to everyone who suffered injury and distress today and to their families.'

Merlin's crisis management response, based on a culture that allowed effective communication to take place and a leadership team that was prepared to do and say the right things quickly, could only have been executed with planning and exercising beforehand.

Summary

History shows that a mishandled crisis has a major impact, not just on the value and reputation of the organisation in question, but also on the lives and livelihoods of the stakeholders who are affected by it. Despite this, we continue to see the same mistakes made by leaders of businesses as they struggle to take control of a crisis.

Their missteps are sometimes due to cultural or structural factors associated with the business itself but just as often they are due to the unique characteristics of a crisis.

Dealing with the complexities of a crisis requires planning, training and exercising before the event. Investing time and effort in these areas may even prevent a crisis in the first place.

Questions

- What could your business lose if you mishandled a crisis? What is at stake?

- Which stakeholders could be affected if your business had a crisis?

- Which stakeholders could influence the business and reputational impact of a crisis on your business?

- What are the potential impacts on your stakeholders should you mishandle a crisis?

- How quickly could you communicate with your stakeholders if a crisis happened right now?

- What plans do you currently have in place to help you make good decisions under pressure?

TWO

How To Create A Robust Crisis Management Framework

'By failing to prepare, you are preparing to fail.'
— Benjamin Franklin

Your CEO asks to see you about an 'opportunity'. They tell you they're concerned that the business is unprepared to manage a major crisis and could be seriously damaged should the worst occur.

Given the success of your business and its positive reputation, that's a big worry and it needs addressing. It's not only important for the business but also to ensure that the lives and livelihoods of its stakeholders – employees, communities, customers, investors, suppliers – are protected.

They want you to establish and maintain a comprehensive programme of crisis preparedness. They know you already have more than enough on your plate with your main area of responsibility but have nevertheless selected you to lead this area. Your energy, commitment and ability to cut through bureaucracy mean you are the person they trust to get this critical job done. They need someone with the determination to make a real difference to protecting your business, not someone who will simply 'tick the boxes'.

You are flattered, and your passion for the business means it's a responsibility that motivates you. Yet there are nagging questions at the back of your mind: where do I start? How will I know what to do? What if I take us in the wrong direction? What if I omit a critical part of the planning process?

Even worse: what happens to the business (and me) if we mishandle a crisis as a result of a flaw in the crisis management programme for which I am responsible?

As Stagecoach's Steven Stewart observed: 'It is the only time in my career that I have been able to understand what it must feel like to be the CEO of an organisation. There's a huge weight of responsibility on your shoulders.'

These fears are entirely understandable and are common to most nonspecialist crisis managers who are made accountable for a programme of crisis preparedness.

However, there is also a sense of privilege and legacy when one takes on this role, as Stephen Covey, Chief Security Officer at Canadian National Railways, reflects: 'The opportunity to take on a project that will have a long-term impact and be of real benefit to the company made the challenge really attractive to me.'

Sue Boxall, who as vice president of HR at Lundin Mining Corporation was given responsibility for implementing a new crisis management programme, concurs:

> 'Crisis management can be rather daunting for
> someone new to the role. But with the active
> support of your CEO plus clear direction and
> commitment from the senior team, then this is
> a very rewarding role and should be enjoyed.'

This chapter sets out some of the building blocks of crisis management to begin your crisis planning programme from firm foundations. It removes some of the mystique about crisis management and sets out its relationship with areas such as business continuity and emergency response planning.

Understanding your brief and the scope of crisis management is the essential first step to building a comprehensive and robust programme of activity.

What is crisis management?

When I speak with businesspeople and ask them what they understand by 'crisis management', there's little consistency in how they respond. This is not surprising as few of them are specialists in this area.

But, as someone who has been tasked with leading a crisis management preparedness programme, you need to know precisely what it means for *your* business. More than that, your fellow executives must share the same understanding. Without this clarity and single mindedness, which are so essential in a crisis, you are creating a recipe for an even bigger disaster.

A common lexicon is required to understand what crisis management is, what it isn't and how it differs from interrelated disciplines.

In its publication 'Crisis management – Guidance for developing a strategic capability', the British Standards Institute (BSI) defines a crisis as 'an unprecedented or extraordinary event or situation that threatens an organisation and requires a strategic, adaptive, and timely response in order to preserve its viability and integrity'. It defines crisis management as 'the development and application of the process, systems, and organisational capability to deal with crises'.

We'll come on to how you define a crisis for your business in Chapter 8 (How To Develop Your Crisis

Management Plan) but for now here is an example from a real crisis management plan for a large, well-known consumer-facing business which operates across Europe: 'A crisis is a sudden event or escalating issue that may significantly affect our reputation and/or our ability to carry out our business.' The business in question describes its crisis management objective as 'Maintaining the long-term trust, confidence and support of all our stakeholders'.

Crisis management is how you prepare for and respond to a major situation with the intention of maintaining the long-term trust of those with a stake in the business and thereby protecting business value and reputation. Because crisis management focuses on business value and reputation and is designed to preserve the long-term confidence of all its stakeholders, it is by definition a strategic activity.

The natural implication of this is that it demands active involvement by senior management. Responsibility cannot be delegated (though some tasks can). Your success as the champion for crisis management within your business relies upon the active involvement of your senior colleagues, a topic which we will return to in Chapter 4 when we explore ways of securing executive buy-in.

How does crisis management fit with interrelated areas?

Crisis communication

As shown by the definitions of crisis management above, protecting reputation is a key objective when responding to a crisis, and communication is a critical means of achieving this. Making the right decisions about who you communicate with, what you say, when and how will be essential if you are to retain stakeholder trust and confidence.

This does not mean that effective communication is enough on its own to successfully manage a crisis. Far from it. To emerge from a crisis intact, businesses must do two things simultaneously: fix whatever problem lies at the heart of the crisis (the operational response) while at the same time communicating effectively with the many stakeholders affected by the situation. This is the only way of guaranteeing the protection of business value and reputation. One without the other is never enough.

Understanding this is critical. Too often I have seen businesses produce 'crisis management plans' that are nothing of the kind. They are simply crisis *communication* plans. Consequently, the business is inadequately prepared to respond fully to a crisis.

Remember: communication is an essential part of your crisis response, but it is never the whole story. Beware crisis communication plans masquerading as crisis management plans.

Business continuity management

The international standard for business continuity (ISO 22301) defines it as the 'capability of an organization to continue the delivery of products or services within acceptable time frames at predefined capacity during a disruption'.

Business continuity focuses on keeping your business running despite the disruption caused by an incident. That requires your business to pre-plan which functions are most critical, who your essential team members are and strategically significant customers.

Having completed this analysis (known as a 'business impact analysis' or BIA) the company can then plan contingencies for a potential disruption. Solutions can include, for example, alternative workplaces, disaster recovery for IT systems and manual workarounds to address system failures.

Business continuity management is required when responding to many crisis types (especially those that are operationally focused such as fires, floods, IT outages, supply chain issues or terrorist incidents) but it is only part of the whole crisis management effort.

While continuing to operate in the short term is undoubtedly important, the role of crisis management focuses on the longer-term viability of the business by retaining the trust and confidence of its stakeholders.

Risk management

In its ISO Guide 73, the International Organization for Standardization defines risk management as 'coordinated activities to direct and control an organization with regard to risk'.

Risk management begins with the identification, evaluation and prioritisation of risks and is followed by activity to minimise, monitor and control the probability or impact of key risks. As such, it forms an important part of crisis management.

In Chapter 6 we will consider how to assess your risk landscape and identify your priority risks.

An understanding of your risk landscape forms an important part of your crisis management planning, but don't allow it to create tunnel vision, warns Cathay Pacific's Gus Whitcomb:

'Visibility of your risk profile helps to shape your crisis management planning, but it should never constrain it. Beware the crisis management plan which limits itself to those pre-identified risks which your management team can conceive of. If you cannot think the unthinkable, at least have a plan which is designed to manage the unthinkable.'

Emergency response

The Ready campaign, a United States government initiative designed to educate the American people on how to prepare for and respond to emergencies, describes the purpose of an emergency response plan as follows:

'When an emergency occurs, the first priority is always life safety. The second priority is the stabilization of the incident. There are many actions that can be taken to stabilize an incident and minimize potential damage. First aid and CPR by trained employees can save lives. Use of fire extinguishers by trained employees can extinguish a small fire. Containment of a small chemical spill and supervision of building utilities and systems can minimize damage to a building and help prevent environmental damage.'

As illustrated above, emergency response is about the immediate response to an incident and focuses on the preservation of life, the environment and property (in that priority order). It is entirely tactical and operational in nature and includes, for example, how to evacuate people.

Not all emergencies are crises: sometimes an emergency is quickly resolved and never escalates into a crisis. On other occasions, emergency response is required during the early stages of a crisis, perhaps for the first few hours, before the emergency phase concludes. Even in these situations, the initial emergency response does not constitute the entire crisis management effort: it is simply one important element of it. Broader crisis management activity will take place in parallel.

Remember: crisis management activity is strategic and focused on the long term. Emergency response is tactical and focuses on the immediate term.

Jim French, Vice President, Health, Safety and Risk at Lundin Mining, sums it up neatly:

> 'The best way to think about it is that emergency responders work at 10 feet, the site crisis management teams at 10 thousand feet, and senior corporate leadership at 30 thousand feet.

> 'Emergency responders are out on the ground controlling whatever the immediate risk, whether that's dealing with the rescue, triaging patients, or fighting fires.

'The crisis team looks at the bigger picture, plans further ahead, and coordinates the overall effort. They will be addressing issues such as: "We had an issue at the plant. There's a smoke cloud. What is it? Where's the smoke cloud going? What are the risks? Who might be affected? What do we need to do? Who do we need to notify?" Or, "Material has spilled into the environment. What is it? What are the risks or impacts? Who or what could be impacted? What do we need to do? Who do we need to communicate with?"

'It's also the responsibility of the crisis management team to ensure that the emergency responders get the supplies, support, and other resources they need to respond to an incident effectively and safely.'

The four essential pillars of crisis preparedness

This book will help you prepare for a corporate nightmare: a major crisis striking your business. Being able to do and say the right things under pressure requires you to address the following four areas of crisis preparedness.

1. **Assess:** given the unpredictable nature of a crisis, it can be difficult to know where to start

in protecting your business and its reputation. Reviewing your current capability and identifying the threats your business faces and their potential impact is the perfect foundation for a crisis management programme.

Assessing your crisis landscape gives you the understanding and foresight to effectively protect your business.

2. **Plan:** when businesses react too slowly to a crisis, it is usually because of a lack of crisis management planning. Under enormous pressure, the business is required to muddle through based on instinct and the collective experience of the senior management team. This is rarely a recipe for success. Planning for a crisis gives you the foundations for a swift and effective response.

3. **Train:** plans play an important part in managing a crisis, but people make or break your response. Everyone from your chief executive through to your call centre operators has a role to play and they all need to know what is expected of them. Team and individual training are essential if everyone is to have the knowledge, capabilities and confidence they need to play their part in an effective crisis response. As they say in the army, 'Train hard, fight easy.'

4. **Exercise:** a crisis is a defining moment in a business's history: the decisions it makes at that time determine its fate. Organisations that have

thoroughly rehearsed their crisis response are much more likely to make the right calls.

Just like any other task, practice makes perfect. Exercises test your crisis management plans and processes to identify gaps, flaws and areas for improvement, which can be addressed in advance of a real crisis. A programme of crisis exercising also rehearses your team and reveals skill gaps and training needs.

Ultimately it builds confidence and capability, resulting in a robust plan and a well-drilled team able to deliver a pitch-perfect response under an intense spotlight.

Summary

Crisis management planning, training and exercising give you the ability to protect the value of your business, its reputation and its stakeholders when crisis strikes.

Crisis management is a strategic task for which the leadership team is responsible. It focuses on the long term.

Other related activities such as business continuity, emergency response and risk management feed into crisis management and it is important to understand what fits where.

As you begin your journey to prepare your business for crisis, be sure that you and your senior management colleagues are clear on the purpose of your crisis management planning. A lack of clarity is the enemy of a successful crisis response.

As Canadian National Railways' Steve Covey so rightly points out:

> 'It's a big and important programme and it's easy to become overwhelmed by the scale of it. So it's important to break it down into individual deliverables with achievable goals and a clear timeline. By having clear expectations and landmarks you can see the progress you are making and keep the team motivated.'

Questions

- How do you feel about having responsibility for crisis management? What excites you about the role? What concerns do you have?

- What do your colleagues say when you ask them to define crisis management?

- What is the purpose of crisis management at your business?

- Who is accountable for crisis management at your business (if not you)?

- Who else plays a part in crisis management or other associated disciplines at your business?

- List all of the current plans, processes and policies related to crisis management in your business.

THREE

Beginning Your Crisis Management Programme

'It's like you're cycling down a steep hill, you're going fast and enjoying yourself so much. The exhilaration of the speed and going down the hill makes you oblivious to the fact there's a sharp bend ahead.'
— Gerald Ratner, former CEO of Ratners

Before embarking on your crisis management programme, you should first identify and review what plans, processes and other resources you already have at your disposal.

You will also need colleagues and advisors to assist and propel you on your crisis management journey. Their support, expertise and willingness to share the workload will enable you to make quicker and more sustainable progress.

This chapter sets out what you should do before activating the crisis management programme itself.

Taking stock

It's unlikely you will embark on your programme of crisis management planning, training and exercising without any pre-existing plans, processes or capability.

As outlined in Chapter 2, you may already have in place resources and policies related to crisis management: maybe business continuity, emergency response or incident management plans. Are they comprehensive, consistent, integrated and sufficient to protect your business and reputation should the worst occur?

You should answer these questions before creating new ways of working in a crisis. To assist in this process, consider benchmarking your current plans against crisis management standards such as the BSI's publication 'Crisis management – Guidance for developing a strategic capability'.

You should also review your plans from the perspective of someone in your business who might have to deploy them under intense pressure. Base your evaluation on the following three criteria for effective crisis management:

- **Completeness:** do you have a comprehensive set of crisis management collateral to facilitate an effective response?

- **Clarity:** is content communicated clearly and simply for easy application under pressure in a crisis?

- **Cohesion:** do plans sit within an overall framework and integrate with each other?

In addition to working through your plans, it's also a good idea to take soundings from colleagues who are either directly involved in crisis management planning (for example, your head of health and safety or your business continuity manager) or who would likely be called upon to play a role in your crisis management team.

Find out how confident they are in your current plans and their ability to successfully execute them. Get their feedback on any training or crisis exercises in which they may have participated. Engaging them in this way not only informs the development of an improved set of resources, it also helps to secure their buy-in to the whole idea of crisis management.

An objective, well-informed assessment of your current level of preparedness, gaps and areas for attention gives you the foundation to better protect your business.

Forming your crisis management taskforce

You may be accountable for your company's crisis management preparedness, but you certainly can't make the business crisis proof without a lot of support from people within, and sometimes outside, your business. Getting the right people on board means you will end up with a well-conceived crisis management programme quicker than would otherwise be possible.

Key internal stakeholders

As Katrin Suesser, Director Legal, Compliance and Corporate Governance at Lidl UK, observes:

> 'In a crisis you need to work collaboratively with colleagues from a range of functions. It's important to build relationships so you understand what they are doing and why. If you start this in a crisis then it's probably too late.'

Begin your crisis management planning by involving the following people from inside your business.

- **Board of directors/chief executive/managing director:** crisis management only ever gets the attention it deserves if it has the full, genuine and explicit support of its leader. As Stagecoach's

Steven Stewart points out: 'If the leader of your organisation does not buy into the importance of crisis management and communications, then you will never effectively manage a crisis. You will be down in the weeds and you won't be focused on the big decisions which will determine the future success of your business.'

Having your CEO championing crisis management, participating in every crisis simulation and demanding the same of their colleagues communicates a powerful message. Enlisting the active and ongoing support of your CEO should be your first priority.

- **General counsel/head of legal:** almost every crisis brings legal implications, so having your senior lawyer on board is essential. Establishing some principles ahead of time (not least approval processes) helps to avoid time-consuming conversations during the heat of a crisis.

- **Head of communication/PR:** crises always have the potential to affect reputation and they invariably require communication with stakeholders, so engaging your head of communication is vital. Find out whether they have existing crisis communication plans or materials in place and how they would upweight their communication resources in the event of a major incident. Make sure the distinction between crisis management and crisis communication is clear to avoid misunderstandings later (see my definitions in Chapter 2).

- **Head of HR:** your people are a critical part of every crisis, whether they are directly affected or interested observers. Depending on the crisis type, HR may have employee relations responsibilities from internal communication to grief counselling. Talk with them to understand their perspective on the people element of crisis management.

- **Head of risk:** crisis is a risk come true, so your head of risk must be part of your crisis planning process. Engage them to help understand your risk profile and use their expertise to inform exercise scenarios.

- **Head of health and safety:** crises in the form of accidents, incidents and physical events will often have health and safety implications. An understanding of your emergency response procedures will help to ensure that health and safety procedures align with your crisis management plans.

- **Head of business continuity:** business continuity is not synonymous with crisis management but it is an important part of it. Avoid fuzziness or contradictions between your business continuity and crisis management plans by closely involving your head of business continuity in the crisis management planning process.

- **Head of ESG/CSR/environment and community:** your attitude to environmental, social and corporate governance (ESG) must be reflected within your approach to crisis management. With reputational risks becoming increasingly important, you should work closely with your head of ESG to ensure that risks related to this area are fully covered in your crisis management programme.

- **Head of information security:** with cyber threats now forming an important part of most businesses' risk landscape, you should collaborate with your head of information security. Make sure that, as well as the technical response to a cyber incident, the strategic response is also covered.

- **Head of security:** threats such as terrorism and kidnapping are often the responsibility of a business's head of security. Ensure that that they are represented in your crisis planning but beware a situation where their focus means that all crisis exercising is focused on security risks.

Use the list above as a starting point for building alliances on your crisis management journey but tailor it to reflect the structure and operations in your business.

Crisis coordinator

While you have accountability for crisis management you will also benefit from a trusted lieutenant in the role of crisis coordinator. They are the person responsible for critical tasks such as:

- Updating the crisis management plan and notifying the team of any changes

- Ensuring that new members of the senior team are briefed on the plan

- Scheduling crisis management training and exercising

- Updating contact details

- Checking the requirements of your crisis management policy have been met

- Ensuring the crisis management team have all the resources they require

- Maintaining the crisis management team room

- Keeping 'go-bags' stocked

The person you select for this role should be utterly reliable and trustworthy, well organised, professional and tenacious. Given that you will work collaboratively on the crisis management programme, they should be someone with whom you can work effectively. They will also have responsibilities during the crisis which we will return to in Chapter 10 (Creating An Effective Crisis Management Team).

Specialist partners and advisors

As you develop and maintain your crisis management planning, training and exercising programme you may need specialist external support from time to time. While there is a cost to employing third parties, their experience, expertise and objectivity can add significant value (not least in securing the attention of your senior colleagues and, as outsiders with no vested interest, the ability to give tough feedback when exercising).

Consider the following types of partners as part of your crisis planning, training and exercising team.

- **Business continuity firms:** some business continuity firms also have crisis management capabilities and can assist with planning, training and exercising. Be clear on your expectations in your brief and take up references to ensure they have the expertise you need.

- **Crisis management consultancies:** specialist crisis management firms bring their experience of helping businesses prepare for and handle crises to guide you through the planning process. Most businesspeople only deal with a true crisis once or twice in a career; crisis management consultancies are working with them every day and so know what works and what doesn't.

- **Cyber security consultancies:** if cyber incidents are high on your list of risks, you may wish to engage a cyber specialist firm. They can help with services such as penetration testing and incident response. Identify your requirements, establish whether their expertise is technically or strategically focused and appoint accordingly.

- **PR agencies:** PR agencies can help with your crisis communication planning and execution. Make sure they understand the difference between crisis management and crisis communication, and that their expertise meets your needs. Consider whether you might want agency staff to supplement your in-house PR team in the event of a crisis and make decisions on the size of agency you appoint with this in mind.

Finding the right partners to help support you on your crisis management journey can be challenging. It's a business-critical area with exposure to the most senior people in your organisation so naturally you want to appoint the best partner for your business.

To help you make the right decision, consider:

- Asking for recommendations from peers you trust
- Requesting credentials from your long list of firms

- Issuing a clear and comprehensive brief outlining your objectives, the expertise, capabilities and characteristics you require

- Meeting them face to face for a discussion of their proposal

- Evaluating responses based both on the quality of their response and how they interact with you during the selection process (chemistry and cultural fit is important)

- Taking client references for your preferred partner

Canadian National Railways' Steve Covey underlines the importance of a robust process:

'Obviously, your consultancy partner must have the necessary technical expertise but just as important is their fit with your business and your team. The relationship is so important. You need to talk with them, ideally face to face and get to understand how they will work with you. It's similar to hiring someone for a permanent job. If they will be working with specific team members, I'll fix for those people to meet them to make sure the fit is there. If not, it simply won't work.'

In addition to support during the pre-crisis phase, you will undoubtedly require additional resource should a crisis strike. Work through your risk profile to identify exactly what expertise you may require but consider the following as a starting point:

- Advertising agency
- Call centre capability
- Crisis management specialists
- Cyber specialists
- Designers
- Disaster recovery providers
- Legal advisors
- Media and social media monitoring agency
- PR advisors
- Product testing specialists
- Scientific or technical experts
- Environmental specialists
- Security experts
- Trauma/grief counsellors
- Video production companies

Advisors, like the ones above, are crucially important in a crisis and leadership teams should build a strong group of advisors they trust ahead of the crisis. As NFU Mutual's head of reputation Jo Lumani says: 'Having a third-party perspective on what you're doing well, and areas where you can improve, provides real value for businesses.'

You must also build relationships between the advisors, especially your legal and communication advisors. In the heat of a crisis, you must avoid the potential tug of war between communicators and lawyers, with the communicators advising, 'Tell them everything and tell it now,' while your lawyers recommend, 'Tell them nothing. No comment is the answer.'

One of the ways of avoiding that impasse (or even outright conflict) is building relationships ahead of time. Do this by walking through scenarios with your lawyers, communicators and the other advisors present to hammer out how you would deal with these high-risk situations. This approach – scenario planning – is a topic I cover in more detail in Chapter 7.

Ultimately, though, leaders must understand that while appointing great advisors is a smart move, they cannot hide behind them. In a crisis, you should ask lawyers for their best advice on how to minimise legal risks. Have your communicators give you their recommendations on how to reduce reputational risk. Ask your accountants for their insights on how to contain financial risk.

Listen to their advice, but then it's up to the leader to make the final decision.

This approach was epitomised by Michael McCain, CEO of Maple Leaf, a Canadian producer of cooked meat, which was contaminated with Listeria in 2008. He said:

> 'Going through the crisis, there are two advisors I paid no attention to. The first are the lawyers and the second are the accountants. It's not about money or legal liability. This is about our being accountable for providing customers with safe food.'

Summary

Start your crisis management programme by assessing the resources you already have at your disposal. Evaluate the extent to which plans are complete, clear and cohesive. Canvass the views of colleagues who have involvement in or experience of crisis management: their insights will be valuable.

Identify the critical people whose input and support you will require on your crisis management journey. Appoint a trusted colleague as your crisis coordinator to support you in developing and maintaining your crisis management programme. Consider bringing in specialist advisors to supplement your in-house team.

Questions

- To what extent are your current plans complete, clear and cohesive? What needs to be done to make them better?

- Whose feedback will you secure on the effectiveness of current plans?

- Which internal stakeholders should be part of your crisis management taskforce?

- What external support will you need?

- Who could be your crisis coordinator?

FOUR

How To Secure Executive Buy-In

'I work for a CEO who really gets it. I approached him when he first took over and said to him that we needed to do an annual senior management exercise. He said to me, "No, we don't." When I looked at him kind of strangely, he said, "We need to do at least two of those a year." I'm blessed with somebody who actually understands what needs to be done.'

— Gus Whitcomb, head of crisis management, Cathay Pacific

Some CEOs are naturals when it comes to crisis management. From Michael Bishop, who led British Midland through a major air crash back in 1989, to Richard Branson, who steered Virgin through two crises – a train crash in 2007 and the Virgin Galactic catastrophe in the Mojave desert in 2014 – some leaders instinctively embrace the principles of sound crisis management.

If you are accountable for crisis management, the active engagement of your leadership team makes a huge difference to your chances of success. It instils confidence that in the event of a crisis they will do and say the right things and provides impetus for crisis preparation.

A personally penned foreword and the CEO's signature at the beginning of your crisis management plan is a signal of intent. Their attendance and active participation in crisis simulations are guaranteed to set expectations for others.

As Lundin Mining's Jim French asserts:

> 'There has to be commitment from the board and the C-suite. It takes visible leadership to get the rest of the organisation aboard. Otherwise, your plans are nothing more than a mechanical tool which sits on a shelf and checks a box but doesn't have any real meaning.'

Unfortunately for some executives accountable for crisis management, the active support of their leaders is not a given, but instead must be won. While a regulatory or legal requirement may be the driver for some leaders to commit to crisis management planning and exercising, a compulsion to prepare for crisis is much less powerful than a strongly held desire to do so. Securing executive engagement in crisis management may not be easy, but the benefits in terms of business resilience will be enormous.

The section below outlines tried and tested strategies to get your senior management team on board with crisis management.

Demonstrate the cost of failure

The cost of a crisis can be huge. In the four months after Volkswagen's emissions scandal broke, its value fell by a third. Six months after its data breach in 2017, Equifax's shares were 15% down.

But the cost of crisis is not simply limited to share value. Other significant impacts include:

- Injury or loss of life

- Loss of jobs

- Reputational damage

- Legal consequences

- Fines

- Cost of remedial action

Another big impact is on the business's ability to retain and recruit staff: no one likes to be associated with a tarnished organisation.

However, the single biggest cost is often hidden, and that's management time. A crisis demands management attention, and lots of it. In response to UK bank TSB's crippling service outage in April 2018, its former CEO Paul Pester said: 'I will take direct control from eight o'clock this morning for our platform, I've drafted in a team of global experts from IBM. They are reporting to me, directly to me and I will take control of the platform until it gets fixed. I am putting things right.'

His commitment to lead from the front was laudable (if ultimately unsuccessful), but it underlines the all-consuming demands of a crisis on senior leadership time. Focusing your leadership team's attention on the many costs of crisis can be a powerful way of motivating them to act.

Make it personal

Referring to a sherry decanter sold by his eponymous jewellery chain, Gerald Ratner told the 1991 Institute of Directors' conference: 'People say, "How can you sell this for such a low price?" I say, "Because it's total crap."' The speech and reaction to it not only wiped £500 million pounds off the value of his business, but he was forced out of the company he founded and lost his personal reputation.

In an interview for this book, he told me:

> 'I courted the press: I loved the fact they were talking about the success of Ratners. We suddenly became very successful and I was very proud of that. We were the fastest growing share price on the whole of the stock market for two years running. I was still young, very proud of what we'd achieved. I was getting so much great publicity one minute and then overnight we were getting the exact opposite and I was being dragged through the mire. The press was belittling the company that I had made so successful, the world's largest jewellers. It was just the worst.'

More recently, other CEOs including BP's Tony Haywood and Boeing's Dennis Muilenburg were perceived to have mishandled high-profile crises and ceased to lead their businesses following criticism of their performance.

If corporate harm is insufficient to attract management attention, the personal impact can help to focus minds. No leader wants a botched crisis as a stain on their CV, so a subtle appeal to their self-interests can help to attract their attention. Everyone cares about their personal reputation and, when a crisis occurs, executive reputation and credibility are in serious jeopardy. Getting your senior colleagues to focus on that fact can be motivating in ensuring they commit to crisis management planning.

Communicate the broader benefits

It's understandable if executives balk at a significant time and financial investment in crisis management planning: no one likes paying for insurance. However, the belief that crisis management planning and training only have value if the worst occurs is flawed. In fact, engaging in crisis management planning, training and exercising can have huge benefits on business as usual.

Firstly, crisis management planning and training reduce the likelihood of an incident occurring. The crisis planning process reveals vulnerabilities that can be addressed and creates greater vigilance to identify early signs of a potential crisis.

Secondly, by developing and rehearsing crisis management plans and processes, the impact of a situation can be much reduced. A well-executed crisis management response based on thorough planning and training can snuff out a problem almost before it emerges.

But the benefits of crisis management training are broader still. Managing information, dealing with uncertainty, communicating clearly, leadership, team-work and decision-making are all capabilities that are developed under pressure through crisis exercises. The fact they are trained and rehearsed in a pressurised environment means they are deeply embedded and can be effectively deployed in a business-as-usual situation.

As Aoife Clarke, Head of Communications at Lidl Ireland, says:

> 'Even when managing a situation which is not a crisis, people refer back to our crisis management training and the principles which underpin our plan. They will say, for example, "Let's use the Four Boards to organise our thinking about this situation," or "So what's our strategic objective in managing this situation?"'

Communicating the broader benefits of crisis management training and its relevance to day-to-day business challenges can reframe the investment decision.

Get your timing right

Like anything in life, timing is critical to success. Here are some of the occasions when you are more likely to get a positive response to your request for senior management attention on crisis management planning and training.

- **Corporate change:** change usually brings with it significant risk. Awareness of the potential downsides of a change programme can make leaders more receptive to risk management activity.

- **External developments:** external drivers and events can spark interest in crisis management planning. Recent examples include COVID-19, cybercrime and terrorism. Be aware of how the outside world is changing and its potential to act as a catalyst for crisis management planning and training.

- **Competitor issues:** sometimes a crisis that impacts a competitor provides a spur to redouble your organisation's commitment to crisis management. When a crisis is close to home, a realisation dawns that 'it could have been us'. For example, when the horsemeat scandal occurred in 2013, even food manufacturers unaffected by the incident were prompted to review the integrity of their own supply chains and plan for how they would handle a similar contamination. As Gus Whitcomb says:

'When a crisis happens at a company your CEO admires, that's the time to engage senior management and say, "Hey, look at how those guys handled that. If it was us, I wonder if we would have been able to do the same kind of thing that they did? I know we think of them as a good role model. Should we make some changes to be ready to handle things the same way that they did?"'

- **Near misses:** from time to time, organisations avoid a full-scale crisis by the skin of their teeth. In the immediate aftermath, some take a deep breath and quickly return to business as usual. The more enlightened view this as a narrow escape and vow to be better prepared should such an incident recur in future. Make the most of this window of opportunity when leaders recognise the potential impact of crisis and the requirement to be ready to respond.

- **Budget cycles:** crisis management planning and training can be one of those important but rarely urgent tasks that is all too easily side-lined. As a consequence, you may need to be opportunistic when pitching for investment. It can be easier to secure funding for crisis management planning towards the end of the financial year when some budgets are under-spent, especially if the budget in question falls under the 'use it or lose it' category.

Build alliances with like-minded colleagues

If you feel like a lone voice extolling the virtues of crisis management, identify and build relationships with peers who share a similar agenda.

Find colleagues who have a stake in risk management and work together to communicate the benefits of thorough crisis management. Presenting a united front can add credibility and a broader focus to your discussions with senior leaders.

Look out also for senior champions, people who may not be explicitly responsible for this area but who take it seriously and have influence over their peers. Use them as advocates for crisis management.

Start small and grow

Expecting your leadership team to sign off a comprehensive programme of crisis management planning, training and exercising can sometimes be a tall order.

Instead, an incremental approach can be more effective. Try to make the first stage an activity which both enhances your crisis resilience and also secures the team's engagement. Two tried and trusted ways of meeting these criteria are reputational risk assessments (covered in more detail in Chapter 6) and scenario planning workshops (Chapter 7).

A reputational risk assessment opens the team's eyes to the range of risks that the organisation faces. As such, it can be an effective wake-up call to a team in danger of sleepwalking unprepared into a crisis.

Alternatively, a scenario planning workshop requires executives to consider how they would respond to a likely crisis scenario. Identifying gaps in your ability to respond – whether resources or capability – can be the precursor to a bigger programme of planning and training.

Reputational risk assessments and scenario planning workshops can be an effective launchpad for a much bigger programme of crisis management planning *and* the catalyst for continued executive engagement.

Deploy trusted third parties

It can be frustrating to continually communicate the benefits of robust crisis management if it feels like no one is listening. Sometimes it helps for executives to hear the same message from a different source.

Using trusted third parties to communicate the value and importance of crisis management planning and training can help to seal the deal. Non-executive directors – especially those who have endured crises of their own – can be particularly powerful advocates for a programme of crisis management planning and training. Their credibility and influence with the executive team should not be underestimated.

Equally, there will be informal influencers who you know have the ear of your CEO or other key players within the leadership team. Can you bring them into your confidence and make them advocates for the programme you are developing? Building relationships with people who can influence senior leaders can be helpful.

As an alternative, consider using crisis management consultants to communicate the rationale for crisis preparedness. Sometimes the voice of an expert third party can secure the go-ahead for a project that had been previously shelved or vetoed.

Get your own house in order first

Sometimes, despite your best efforts, it remains difficult to secure the full engagement and active involvement of your leadership team. If so, you may choose to focus your energy on areas within your control.

For example, if you are responsible for communication, make sure you have the necessary resources in place to communicate effectively in a crisis. Train your media spokespeople, draft template holding statements, run best practice sessions for your team and organise your own mini exercises. Build relationships with peers with whom you may need to collaborate in a crisis, not least colleagues in HR and legal. Take time to agree the approval process and, for example, discuss with your HR peers how an employee fatality would be communicated.

Whatever your area of responsibility, there are things you can do independently to be ready to respond to a breaking crisis. There is no substitute for senior management commitment to crisis management, but in the absence of this, you can at least put some of the key building blocks in place.

Summary

Crises are most likely to be prevented or handled well if a crisis-resistant culture is deeply embedded within the organisation. This is dependent upon the active involvement and support of your senior team.

If you are fortunate enough to work with a CEO who naturally engages with crisis management, then this should naturally develop. Where this is not the case, deploying some of the strategies outlined above will help to secure their full commitment.

As Sue Boxall explains, the achievement of executive engagement is an important indicator of the degree to which crisis management is embedded within your organisation:

> 'How will you know if your crisis management programme is successful? One sure way of knowing that your business is fully engaged is when senior people within the organisation request a training event or an update on crisis management planning.'

Questions

- Whose support is essential if your crisis management programme is to succeed?

- How engaged are they currently?

- What strategies will you deploy to secure executive buy-in?

- Who can assist with this process?

- What are the first three things you will do to secure the engagement of key colleagues?

SECTION TWO
ASSESS

FIVE

Crisis Culture

> 'Boeing's economic incentives led the company to a significant lack of transparency with the Federal Aviation Administration, its customers, and 737 MAX pilots regarding pilot training requirements and negatively compromised safety.'
> — US Congressional Report, 'The Design, Development and Certification of the Boeing 737 MAX', September 2020

Some crises are completely unpredictable and unpreventable. Some, but not many. Even then, there are steps you can take to reduce their impact.

By creating a crisis-resistant culture you can reduce the likelihood of a crisis occurring in the first place and be ready to respond quickly and effectively to the first signs of a problem.

Crisis management planning, training and exercising are all essential elements of reputation protection. However, creating a crisis-resilient culture is the critical first step.

As Sue Boxall points out:

> 'Crisis management should be embraced, not feared or put into the "too difficult" box. It must become part of "the way we do business" and be embedded into the culture of the organisation. It really is the only way to reduce incidents happening in the first place.'

This chapter outlines the structures, attitudes, values and behaviours that leave organisations vulnerable to a crisis-prone culture, and the steps that can be taken to address them.

Recognising a crisis-prone culture

Beware the following cultural traits, which could leave you more vulnerable to a crisis.

A centralised, hierarchical culture

Successful crisis management requires swift decision-making and action to address a rapidly developing situation. The people best placed to make decisions and take action are those nearest to the crisis.

Organisations – especially international businesses operating across multiple continents and time zones – with a centralised structure and a strict hierarchy are likely to deliver a suboptimal crisis management response.

That's because a culture in which head office dictates decisions and actions, and whose approval is always required, will likely respond more slowly and with actions that fail to address the real situation on the ground.

Many commentators have suggested this was a factor in Toyota's mishandling of its 2010 global product recall, triggered by a potentially lethal accelerator fault on its vehicles. The company's hierarchical approach to management is cited as one of the causes of a delay in identifying and addressing the situation before it became a full-blown crisis.

Where layers of a hierarchy fail to communicate quickly and openly with one another, junior employees, who are best placed to spot early signs of crisis, will be reticent to point out flaws. As in the case of Toyota, this leads to problems going unnoticed and unresolved until they explode into a major crisis.

To avoid this trap, create a culture, structure and crisis management plan that allow local executives to make quick decisions in a crisis without having to turn to head office to approve their every move. The corporate body should be there to support the front line and provide strategic direction, not dictate to it.

Substandard governance

Some of the most damaging crises occur when there has been a failure of effective organisational governance. Historically, Enron is perhaps the best (worst) example. More recently, FIFA and Volkswagen have suffered major reputational harm due to a lack of effective governance.

Self-inflicted crises are usually the most damaging of all as they strike at the heart of the organisation's integrity and competence. Ensure that your governance structures meet best practice and are scrupulously followed to avoid potentially cataclysmic damage.

Inability to challenge people of high status or power

In January 2020, internal emails sent by Boeing employees before the fatal 737 MAX crashes were released by US congressional investigators. They revealed a culture in which frontline employees felt unable to express their concerns about safety. One included the comment: 'I still haven't been forgiven by God for the covering up I did last year. Can't do it one more time. Pearly gates will be closed.'

As Scott Hamilton, aviation analyst at Leeham Company, points out in a 2019 *Sunday Times* article: 'When you create a culture of pressure, where engineers and pilots feel they cannot bring up safety concerns because of cost and timing pressures because of their jobs, that's a culture that emanates from the top.'

Domineering senior executives whose word is law create the breeding ground for a crisis. Their view that a project is safe to proceed will always carry the day, even when colleagues have concerns. Unfortunately, in a culture like this, employees with an alternative perspective will be too frightened to express their concerns, or simply not bother because they know they will not be listened to.

This scenario relates not just to people at the top of the organisational hierarchy; it can also apply to star performers. They could be, for example, the leading salesperson or the creative hotshot: their commercial value to the organisation is deemed to be so great that challenges to their views or behaviours are never made.

Star performers and charismatic CEOs can be tremendous assets to a business, but they must still align with the overall culture, and they should never be untouchable.

Misguided incentivisation or target setting

Give a person an incentive or measure them against a particular target and they will respond accordingly. As a consequence, organisations must ensure that incentives or targets that make good business sense do not introduce unacceptable risk as a consequence.

For example, the pursuit of unrealistically high sales targets can result in unethical practices or falsification of numbers. Sky-high production targets can cause operators to cut corners, leading to health and safety risks.

In another email sent before the 737 MAX crashes, a Boeing employee said: 'I don't know how to fix these things…it's systemic. It's culture. It's the fact we have a leadership team that understand very little about the business and yet are driving us to certain objectives.'

Make sure your incentives and objectives do not lead to unintended consequences in the form of increased vulnerability to crisis.

It could never happen here

If you believe you are immune to crisis you will never invest in crisis management planning or training, leaving yourself powerless to respond should the worst occur. Ironically, some of the best-run organisations can suffer from this syndrome. They believe their quality systems, health and safety procedures and esteemed reputation protect them from harm. In short, they fall into the trap of believing their own PR.

No organisation is immune from crisis, and recognition of this is essential to create a crisis-resilient culture. One of the best ways of surfacing this issue is by running a reputational risk assessment (explained in more detail in Chapter 6). In doing so, take a look at your organisation from the outside (rather than from inside the corporate bubble) to understand your true level of vulnerability.

Over-confidence in your ability to respond

Even where there is recognition that a crisis could occur, there may be a belief that the rigour of an organisation's processes and the qualities of its people would enable it to defuse the crisis quickly. This over-confidence results in a lack of thorough crisis management planning, training and testing.

An effective first step in addressing this situation is to engage in scenario planning (see Chapter 7) whereby executives spend time considering situations that could affect your business and work through how they would respond. As they probe their response, it usually becomes clear there are missing links in the chain and additional resources or capabilities are required. Without the foresight to consider the 'what ifs', these gaps only become apparent during a crisis, with the potential for catastrophic results.

Lack of empowerment

The best form of crisis management is crisis prevention, and the best place to prevent a crisis is at the front line. In his report into the Thomas Cook crisis, in which two young children died in a Corfu villa in 2006, Justin King highlighted the need for resort representatives to be empowered to resolve problems at source.

This principle applies to all businesses. Give your frontline staff – call centre operators, sales executives, store assistants and so on – the freedom, knowledge and tools to identify and address issues *before* they become crises.

As Lidl's Aoife Clarke says:

> 'Crisis management can be viewed as a slightly scary or taboo topic, but we've shown that it's just about being prepared and nothing to be afraid of. We encourage our people to raise issues before they become a crisis which allows us to deal with them more proactively.'

Remember also to give these frontliners training in what to do and say in the event of a crisis emerging.

It's all very well having a comprehensive corporate crisis management plan, but if the guy in the front line doesn't know what to do or who to tell it counts for nothing.

Denial or wilful ignorance

You can't manage a crisis if you don't recognise you are facing one.

Managers must beware of wearing blinkers that prevent them from seeing things as they really are. Encouraging whistle blowers, employing external advisors who challenge the conventional wisdom and spending time 'on the shopfloor' are all good ways of avoiding these traps.

Crucially, when an issue arises, leaders must have a mindset that allows them to believe that something can have gone wrong. It is only by recognising the issue that they can begin to address it.

In a front page article in April 2020 headlined 'Coronavirus: 38 days when Britain sleepwalked into disaster', the *Sunday Times* made the case that denial was a significant factor in preventing a swifter response to the outbreak of COVID-19 in the UK.

The ability to identify and react quickly to a crisis can also be enhanced through a regular programme of exercising. It creates a mindset that allows executives to countenance the potential for crisis and to recognise the warning signs. It also means they can react more quickly and effectively should an issue emerge.

Blaming crises on human error

In February 2016 two trains collided head on near Bad Aibling in southern Germany, killing twelve people and injuring many more. The accident occurred when the train dispatcher gave incorrect orders to the two trains. Having realised his error, he compounded it by trying to send emergency codes to the trains but entered the wrong combination. The prosecutor who investigated the crash concluded it was caused by human error.

While his finding is understandable, if you want to be truly crisis resistant beware such a simplistic conclusion.

Organisations that put the cause of a crisis entirely down to human error are unlikely to seek out and learn lessons around the deeper factors that led to it, leaving themselves vulnerable to future crises. You must look beyond the ultimate human action or inaction that was the final catalyst for a crisis.

Identify the conditions, causes and pressures that led to someone making a bad decision. Underlying factors can include, for example, a lack of training or briefing, inadequate quality or safety systems, or pressure to achieve goals (productivity, speed or financial) that could compromise safety.

To avoid this fate, organisations should conduct a full and objective post-crisis review of the underlying causes and identify key learnings. Involving a third party to lead the investigation can provide the external perspective and objectivity to see things that insiders can't. Crucially, learning and actions from the review must be acted upon to reduce the likelihood of a repeat incident. We will examine this in more detail in Chapter 15.

Summary

There are many steps that an organisation can take to ensure it is ready to do and say the right thing in the event of a crisis. Crisis management planning, training, exercising and testing often form the heart of this.

All of these steps are important but underpinning everything must be the creation of a crisis-resilient culture. Get that part right and everything else will follow.

Questions

Consider the following questions. If you can answer 'yes' to any of them you may be creating a crisis-prone culture.

- Do some parts of your organisation tend to keep bad news under wraps rather than escalate the issue?

- Is head office responsible for all decision-making in a major crisis?

- Does your organisation accommodate maverick employees who may break the rules from time to time but deliver stellar results?

- Are your people primarily incentivised based on hard numeric targets such as sales, production figures and cost reduction?

- Would your CEO/MD thank a colleague for alerting them to bad news?

SIX

How To Assess Your Risk Landscape

'Risk comes from not knowing what you're doing.'
— Warren Buffett

The crisis management planning, training and exercising programme for which you are responsible must deliver the capability to respond successfully to any crisis type.

A set of risk-specific checklists do not on their own constitute a crisis management plan.

However, understanding your risk landscape *does* enable you to prevent and plan for critical risks as an important part of your crisis planning programme. This chapter explains how to identify and prioritise them.

Why understanding your risk landscape is important

The best crisis management is crisis prevention. Failing that, the next best solution is crisis preparation. Both can be facilitated through risk assessment.

Being aware of your risk landscape (the potential crises your business faces) allows you to take steps to reduce their likelihood of occurrence and prepare contingencies should the risk arise.

It also plays an important part in shaping your crisis management planning, training and exercising programme. Priority risks will have their own response checklists in your crisis management plan. Risk-specific statements and social media content should be part of your crisis communication plan. Your response to high priority risks can be rehearsed through exercises.

Do be aware of the limitations of risk assessment. It is an inexact science and business history is littered with 'black swan' events that have fallen outside of predicted risks and caused havoc as a result.

Equally, do not fall into the trap of ignoring low likelihood, high impact risks. By their very nature, the most devastating crises – huge environmental incidents, major terrorist attacks, catastrophic accidents resulting in mass fatalities – are rare. However, planning for the worst-case scenario is an essential part of effective crisis management.

Building a picture of your risk landscape

Risk registers should cover the full range of threats to an organisation. Sadly, they are often skewed or incomplete. For example, traditional risk management tends to focus on financial risk. Manufacturers, infrastructure and process-driven businesses often major on operational or technical risk. Organisations where security professionals lead crisis management may focus their attention disproportionately on terrorism, kidnap and extortion risks.

All the above risk types are valid, but, as the person responsible for a crisis management programme to protect your entire business, a more holistic perspective of your risk landscape is required.

If your business has already completed risk assessments of one kind or another, review them and evaluate how effectively they cover the full risk landscape faced by your business, including:

- Financial

- Reputational

- Human

- Operational

- Ethical

- Technological

Pay particular attention to the human and reputational risks as these are the ones most commonly overlooked. They are harder (and sometimes more uncomfortable) to identify and assess, but history shows they are often the most damaging types of risks.

News International's phone hacking scandal in 2011 caused the UK's most popular newspaper, the *News of the World*, to cease to exist. Volkswagen's emissions scandal was a crisis focused on corporate ethics and led to enormous damage to one of the world's most trusted and successful automotive brands. Allegations of child labour have threatened the good name of businesses including Nike and Primark.

None of these examples were incident-related: there were no accidents, explosions, fires, environmental incidents or terrorist attacks. They were to do with behaviours, customer service issues, management ethics, culture and integrity.

Ultimately, crisis management is a strategic activity focused on protecting the most precious parts of your business, not least your reputation. Your understanding of risk must reflect this.

Identifying reputational risk

Protecting your organisation requires an understanding of reputational risk as it uniquely relates to your business.

Running a reputational risk assessment teases out not just operational risks, but also the more damaging reputational threats that otherwise remain buried within the organisation. It also prioritises them to create a structured framework for crisis management planning.

How does a reputational risk assessment differ from a conventional risk assessment?

Simply, it looks at the extent to which a risk could damage your reputation by applying a reputational lens and taking an 'outside in' perspective to consider the risk landscape in a slightly different way.

The process works best when a diverse group of executives are brought together for a risk assessment. The HR director brings to the meeting risks related to people, the production director brings those related to manufacturing, and so on. At the session these risks are shared and others are added as part of the brainstorming process.

Identifying risks on the basis of people's personal knowledge and professional expertise is essential. However, it is not enough.

Having exhausted the initial brainstorm, ask your colleagues to step away from their day-to-day role and consider the organisation from an alternative, more challenging perspective.

Ask questions like:

> 'What kind of a crisis could a disgruntled employee cause for us? What kind of a crisis could a really hot investigative journalist create for us? What kind of crisis could our most critical NGO initiate? What is the worst social media storm you could imagine engulfing our business?'

Taking this approach allows executives to be more open-minded and realistic about problems the organisation may face. It will reveal additional risks not identified through a conventional risk assessment.

Having completed the identification exercise, risk prioritisation can follow based on their likelihood of occurrence and potential impact on your business.

In addition to the value of a risk assessment in informing your crisis management planning, the range of risks identified can serve as a wake-up call to sceptical colleagues and secure their engagement with the crisis planning programme.

Identifying killer risks

Ensuring that the reality of your business matches up with its brand promise matters at all times, but it matters most in the event of a crisis.

How do we know this? Well, when Oxford Metrica undertook its analysis of how crises affect the value of businesses, they discovered the biggest value changes occurred when a crisis struck at the heart of the brand. In other words, if the nature of a crisis or how it is handled runs counter to the company's professed positioning, the impact on financial value will be especially severe.

For example, billionaire businessman Richard Branson was subjected to significant criticism as a result of the conflict between his image as a benevolent 'man of the people' and his request for state aid to save his ailing Virgin Atlantic airline in the wake of COVID-19.

Your organisation's values must be much more than skin deep or else it leaves your long-term business value perilously vulnerable to the wrong kind of crisis.

Consider what your business stands for and pinpoint the crisis types that would be particularly damaging to you. If your reputation is built on quality, a crisis related to product defects would be especially harmful. If you're famous for customer care, a crisis in which customers felt ignored or badly treated will be particularly damaging. A company that trumpets its green credentials will be disproportionately harmed by an environmental issue.

You must identify the crisis types that cut across your values and be vigilant to identify and address crises of this kind.

Make sure you understand the characteristics that make your organisation special. And take time to prepare for the crisis types that could put your reputation in jeopardy.

Summary

Understanding your risk landscape is of enormous value in shaping your crisis management programme. Planning for your critical risks provides a head start in responding to many of your most important crisis types, but never place your faith in a crisis management plan that is *only* capable of responding to predictable risks.

Reputational risks can be under-represented in traditional risk registers; consider reputational risk assessments to uncover them, for they have the power to do untold damage to business value and reputation.

Take time to identify and plan for your killer risks, the ones that could bring your business to its knees.

Questions

- Does your business already have a risk register? Does it cover all of your key risk areas including:

  - Financial

  - Reputational

  - Human

  - Operational

  - Ethical

  - Technological

- If not, what is missing?

- What reputational risks could affect your business?

- If you were an investigative reporter, what's the most damaging story you could write about your business?

- What does your business stand for?

- On this basis, what are your 'killer risks'?

- What are your low likelihood, high impact risks?

SECTION THREE
PLAN

SEVEN

How Scenario Planning Can Build Crisis Resilience

'If you've thought through in a nonpressurised situation "If this was to happen, what would we do?", there's a very high chance you'll think correctly and make the right decision at that moment.'
— Former Rugby World Cup winning coach, Sir Clive Woodward

On 27 March 1977, 583 people lost their lives at Tenerife Airport when a KLM jet collided with a PanAm aircraft that was readying itself for take-off on a foggy runway. It remains the worst ever plane crash in terms of fatalities.

Among the sixty-one survivors on the PanAm flight were a married couple named Floy and Paul Heck. As a young man, Paul Heck had been caught up in a fire in a theatre. From that moment on, whenever he entered a crowded place he would always check how to escape, just in case he had the misfortune to be involved in a second incident.

Before the fateful PanAm flight from Tenerife, he sat in his seat and checked the emergency response procedures and listened carefully to the safety briefing by the cabin crew.

When the accident happened, Paul reacted immediately. He stood up, woke his wife and instructed her to get out of her seat, walk down the aisle and jump on to the wing to escape the stricken aircraft.

Paul Heck was one of the few people who had mentally rehearsed what to do if something went wrong. As a consequence, he was ready to react quickly and appropriately when the worst happened. He and his wife owe their lives to his scenario planning.

Businesses should also take time to consider the worst case and how they would respond to it.

What is scenario planning?

Scenario planning enables you to plan for future situations before you experience them for real. It allows you to examine multiple crisis situations and consider alternative response strategies for each.

In a calm and unpressurised environment, it enables you to test your thinking, assess the pros and cons of a range of decisions and identify resources and capabilities required to address each scenario.

In summary, scenario planning is a structured process for considering how your critical risks could play out and determining in advance your optimum response to them.

As Cathay Pacific's Gus Whitcomb describes, scenario planning can be of critical importance when the chips are down:

> 'During 9/11, we were able to work out *what* we were supposed to do. We just didn't have the *how* completely figured out. Which means you have people scrambling, running around trying to figure out how to complete their tasks. For example, who makes any required follow-up phone calls? What are the numbers to call if the delivery systems malfunction? You have to invest time in scenario planning beforehand to get down to the nitty gritty of how something is actually going to function.'

What are the benefits of scenario planning?

Protecting your business under intense pressure means making the right decisions when the heat is on. Scenario planning enables you to rehearse your thinking and decision-making ahead of a crisis and saves time when you need it most. Ultimately, it helps you make the best decisions for long-term reputation protection.

It reveals whether proper processes, checks and safeguards exist and that communication channels have been identified. It enables you to challenge assumptions and probe whether you have the necessary resources to mount a successful crisis management response.

A crisis places extraordinary pressure on your business and its people to do and say the right things. Knowing you have rehearsed your decision-making against critical risks, key processes and resources are in place and the right people are ready to respond is a source of great reassurance. Scenario planning can provide this confidence.

Speaking on the BBC podcast *Don't Tell Me The Score*, Sir Clive Woodward, coach of England's 2003 World Cup winning rugby team, described how T-CUP (Thinking Correctly Under Pressure), his own version of scenario planning, helped his team to successfully overcome pressurised situations. He would provide a clock, a scoreboard and a whiteboard and role play with them:

'I'd bring a player up and say to them: "OK. Scoreboard: England twelve, Australia sixteen – we're four points down. Clock: there's five minutes to go." Then on the whiteboard, I'd set up a situation and ask them: "What would you do?"…'

Take on board Sir Clive's wise advice: think through in advance how you would best react to a challenging situation and you will be much better placed to make the right calls when it happens for real.

As Lidl's Katrin Suesser observes:

'You cannot prepare for a hundred different scenarios but planning for your five most important risk areas has real value. Even when you encounter a different situation, the learnings from scenario planning and training are transferrable and can be applied to whatever you are facing.'

How to run a scenario planning session

To run a scenario planning workshop, you should identify one or more of your critical risks and bring together the group of people responsible for making critical decisions related to each risk. When considering a cyber incident, for example, you might require your chief information security officer, chief operating officer, head of communication, general counsel and head of sales and marketing.

Pre-brief participants on the purpose of the session, risks to be considered and ground rules for the meeting. Develop a short summary of the scenario to be presented to participants at the start of the session.

With the team assembled, either virtually or in a meeting room, remind them of the objectives and ground rules and restate the first scenario to be considered. Let's assume you are an online retailer. The initial scenario presented to the team could be:

> It is now 8.30am on Monday, 18 January 2021. Our data loss prevention system has identified a large file leaving our system. It is clear that hundreds of thousands of customer and employee records may have been affected in the UK, Ireland, Italy and Germany. Data includes customers' phone numbers, emails, addresses and dates of birth, plus employees' home addresses. It is possible that customer financial data has also been compromised but this is not yet confirmed. Country technical teams were activated two hours ago and are investigating the source of the vulnerability, but the exact scope and scale of the breach are still not clear.

Strategic intent

Begin by asking the team, 'What would be our strategic intent in responding to this situation?'

Strategic intent describes the destination you aim to reach by the end of the crisis: it defines your objectives and shapes decisions for all crisis management activity that follows. Your strategic intent is unlikely to change through the duration of the crisis.

Do not move on until you have aligned around a clearly articulated strategic intent for each risk. If a crisis of this type occurs for real, your 'in principle' strategic intent can be quickly reviewed, ratified and used to guide your response.

Top priority

With strategic intent defined, ask, 'What is our top priority right now?' This should be guided by your strategic intent. The purpose of defining your top priority is to focus people, resources and effort on the most important issue at that stage of the crisis. Fail to do this and your response will be dissipated and ineffectual.

Unlike strategic intent, your top priority will change as the crisis evolves. Keep talking until you have landed on a clear statement of your top priority around which the team can align.

Action planning

Ask the team: 'What actions must we take based on our strategic intent and top priority?' Note these down but also interrogate them with two follow-up questions:

- **Why?** – To test and validate your thinking.

- **How?** – To identify resources and capability gaps that need addressing in order for the action to be successfully accomplished. Be careful to identify single points of failure, whether human, operational or technological.

Identify and note down gaps and flaws that could prevent you from managing the situation in the most effective and swift manner. These can be to do with logistics, knowledge, technology, capability or resource: anything that would hinder your response to the crisis should be recorded.

Decision-making

Introduce into the scenario critical decisions that would need to be made. In our example scenario, a key decision could be whether to take down all IT systems. Discuss the pros and cons of alternative decisions and agree 'in principle' decisions.

The purpose of this process is to reduce the thinking time and debate around critical decisions in a real crisis.

It also improves the quality of decision-making as these 'in principle' decisions have been made without the time pressure and high stakes associated with a live crisis. You can also identify criteria or triggers to inform decision-making by agreeing, for example, 'In this kind of crisis, if X happens then we will do Y.'

'In principle' decisions are extremely helpful when your team is under fire during a major crisis. Of course, they should always be tested and ratified against the reality you are facing, but they can save valuable time and facilitate purposeful progress at a time of high stress.

Once discussion has been exhausted and all actions captured, move the scenario on to a new phase. For example, you could tell your team that customers' personal information has now been found for sale on the dark web.

Strategic intent should remain unchanged, but ask again:

- What is our **top priority** right now?

- What **actions** must we take based on our strategic intent and top priority? Why? How? Where are the gaps? Where are the flaws? What actions must we take to address them?

- What **decisions** must we make at this time?

The outputs of your meeting should be used to:

- Create an action plan to address the resource and capability gaps identified

- Confirm strategic intent for key scenarios

- Determine in principle decisions, criteria and triggers for key scenarios

- Develop scenario-specific action checklists for use in a crisis

- Create scenario-specific communication templates (media statements, internal briefings, social media content and so on)

Summary

Scenario planning allows you to identify triggers for business-critical decisions such as when to initiate a product recall, whether to inform customers of a data breach, halt the production line or send staff home in the event of an incident.

It also enables you to surface and address flaws in your crisis response capability, rather than only becoming aware of them during the crisis itself.

Taking the time to conduct scenario planning allows senior managers to make better and quicker decisions in the event of an incident. It also provides greater confidence you have the resources and capabilities you need to prevail in a crisis.

As NFU Mutual's Jo Lumani says:

> 'Scenario planning means that when you
> confront a situation for real, you are better
> prepared, having already walked and talked
> it through. Whatever catastrophe hits your
> business, whether it's a cyber-attack, a fire
> or fatalities, you almost feel like you've been
> through it before.'

Questions

- What are the key scenarios for which you should plan?

- Who should participate in the review of each scenario?

- What is your strategic intent for each of your key scenarios?

- Do you have any single points of failure? What are they?

- Are there learnings from one scenario that are relevant to another?

EIGHT

How To Develop Your Crisis Management Plan

'It's not that pilots are born calm in the face of danger. It's that we review emergency procedures so many times that they come to seem almost routine.'
— Kim Green, writer, public radio producer and pilot

A crisis places your team under extraordinary strain. With incomplete information, limited time, stretched resources and high stakes, you will be challenged to do and say the right things.

Without a well-conceived crisis management plan, the odds of success are stacked against you. According to PwC's 2019 Global Crisis Survey, by a margin of nearly two to one (54% versus 30%), organisations that had a crisis response plan in place fared better post-crisis than those that did not. Equally, those that kept their crisis plan up to date and implemented the lessons learned were four times more likely to come out on top.

A comprehensive, clear and simple crisis management plan ensures your team is focused and purposeful from the minute a crisis breaks.

As Claire Gosnell, Global Head of Brand, Communications and Marketing at international law firm Clifford Chance, says:

> 'A plan provides much needed simplicity in a very complex situation. The checklists and structure it provides allow you to make quicker, more purposeful progress than would otherwise be the case.
>
> 'Basic things like escalation mechanisms, standing agendas and contact details are really helpful. It's so easy to forget something when you're under the pressure of a crisis. Having all that prepared in advance means there's one less thing to worry about.'

The purpose of a crisis management plan

Your crisis management plan should *not* be a step-by-step instruction manual for every conceivable scenario (not least because such a plan would be far too long and unwieldy to use in practice). Equally, teams who expect their plan to provide a blow-by-blow response to their pre-determined risk landscape will be paralysed when a new, unexpected crisis type emerges.

Eilish McGuinness, director for group resilience at media and entertainment company Sky, sums it up neatly:

> 'Crises are not successfully managed by a load of people casually coming together and making it up as they go along. Neither are they managed with a highly detailed playbook. Successful crisis management requires businesses to stand up people quickly, ask the right questions, make decisions, take actions against those decisions, and prioritise communication. If you look at any well-managed crisis situation, you will find it's based on a clear process or structure. That's what makes it a success.'

A good crisis management plan provides a framework for a timely, purposeful and effective crisis response, but it cannot guarantee a successful crisis response.

As Cathay Pacific's Gus Whitcomb recalls when talking about his experience of 9/11:

> 'We went straight to our plan and in about ten seconds realised it wasn't designed for what

we were facing. Our plan was focused on one aircraft, not two. It was focused on one location, not two.

'We had intended to tell our story, one of the basic principles of crisis communications, and yet the very first phone call from the White House was that we shouldn't say a word. And so, all of a sudden, we weren't able to tell our story.

'We planned to fly to the cities where the crisis occurred and help those involved and their families, but all the air traffic was grounded. And so, there we were with this wonderful, beautiful plan that would have worked if we had one airplane in one location, we were able to fly where we were supposed to go and we could tell our story. But it just wasn't the case. And so we had to improvise what we were going to do next. I have to tell you, you don't want to improvise on a crisis of that magnitude.'

Your crisis management plan should not be seen as an inflexible rule book, to be followed to the letter. It provides guidelines and a framework, but every situation is different and every response to a situation will be different.

A crisis management plan can never be a replacement for human judgement (though it should facilitate good decision-making). Even the best crisis management plans cannot guarantee a successful response. They will provide the *framework* for a successful response.

How to develop a plan that works under pressure

Ultimately, crisis management comes down to the skills, abilities and decision-making of people. Your crisis management plan will help you make those decisions and judgements quickly and effectively. But it will not make the decisions for you.

What *should* you expect from your crisis management plan? These are some of the key benefits it should provide when a crisis emerges:

- **Setting you off on the right track** in the vital first hour of a crisis. Fuelled by social media, the speed with which crises emerge and escalate has increased dramatically over recent years. Making good early decisions provides an enormous head start, exerts positive influence over the situation and breeds confidence both within and outside the organisation.

- **Establishing 'battle rhythm':** the rhythm and structure established on day one provides the foundation for what follows. Once you are through the first twenty-four hours, patterns emerge and the team establishes its modus operandi. If your plan is effective in guiding you through those first twenty-four hours, you are already on the road to success.

- **Prioritisation and focus:** a good crisis management plan enables you to prioritise and focus on the most important things first, despite the maelstrom swirling around you.

- **Avoiding omissions or oversights:** checklists are invaluable in a crisis. They act as a safety net when you are under pressure to ensure you don't overlook critical actions.

- **Effective deployment of scarce resources:** in a crisis you never have as much resource as you would like. Making best use of your people is essential. Your crisis management plan should outline key roles and responsibilities, as well as contact details for your 'go to' team members and their deputies.

- **Making good decisions quickly:** decision-making lies at the heart of effective crisis management. While your plan cannot itself make decisions, it should facilitate sound decision-making by giving you the tools to do so.

- **Sound and reliable processes:** a crisis management plan provides a robust framework that you can rely upon at a time of great uncertainty, high stakes and pressure.

Essential content

Your crisis management plan must be tailored to the cultural, organisational and operational realities of your business.

As Lundin Mining's Jim French says:

'Make sure your approach is pragmatic, relevant, and scaled for your business. That way your people can see your approach and your plans fit the business and its operations and are specific to the risks faced. We're a business with five operations and eight different mines. Each one is a little different based on jurisdictional attributes and operating characteristics. While our crisis management plans for each operation have the same basic template, how they are set up and applied varies from operation to operation. Each one is tuned and scaled to the individual operation with additional checklists and site-specific scenarios and protocols.'

A plan structure that works well for one organisation may be completely unsuitable for another. Beware off-the-shelf, 'one size fits all' solutions.

Notwithstanding this, your plan will likely include the following elements.

Foundations

The first section of your plan should set out the foundations of your crisis response. It should be clear, brief and designed to get the right people assembled quickly in response to an emerging issue. It should include the key principles that underpin your crisis response and the steps required to activate your plan and team, in particular:

- **Definition of a crisis:** you can't manage a crisis unless you recognise it's happened. Your crisis management plan must include a definition of what a crisis looks like for your business and what differentiates it from an emergency or lower-level incident. Doing so means that, when your team pulls out the plan, they can quickly identify whether or not they are facing a crisis.

- **Principles for crisis management:** articulating your crisis management principles at the beginning of your plan sets out the basis on which your response should be founded. These principles should be related to your organisational values as well as crisis management best practice. For example, one of our clients simply states: 'Our crisis management response must reflect our core values of responsibility and trust.'

- **Categorisation of crisis types/levels:** some companies categorise crisis types and levels, for example, red, amber and green, or one, two, three according to the severity of the situation. This will have implications for the scale of your response, roles, responsibilities and your approach to communication.

- **Roles and responsibilities:** ensuring that everybody in the organisation knows who is responsible for doing what is a critical first step if your crisis response is to succeed (and an absence of clarity is one of the most common crisis management flaws). It's particularly important if your business is spread across a number of different offices, sites, locations, outlets or countries.

- **Team contact details:** these should be included towards the front of your plan for quick and easy access in a crisis. Remember to also include details for their deputies.

- **Plan and team activation process:** activating your crisis management plan and team is the critical first step to exerting control over a crisis. Doing it quickly and effectively is a top priority. Your plan should set out clearly and simply how the right people will be notified of an incident and attend the initial crisis management team call or meeting.

How to manage a crisis

These are the key mechanics, processes and tasks to ensure the crisis is managed in a purposeful and focused manner. They should always be as clear and simple as possible and include:

- **Overall crisis management process:** an overview, often a table or flowchart, which illustrates your overall approach to crisis management. Simply by looking at this single page, your team should be able to understand the crisis management process they will be applying.

- **Team meeting agenda:** long and unstructured meetings, which end without decisions being made or actions assigned, waste valuable time. By following a standing crisis management team agenda, you have a structure and process for hammering out decisions and actions, enabling the team to purposefully progress its crisis response.

- **First hour action checklist:** a clear, simple checklist of the tasks the team must complete in the first hour is an invaluable prompt to set you off on the right track.

- **Role-specific action checklists:** whether you are the team leader, the spokesperson or loggist, these checklists detail the tasks and actions you should complete (see Chapter 10 for more details on key roles within the crisis management team).

- **Crisis review process:** once the dust has settled and the situation is resolved, it's essential to conduct a full review of what happened to identify what went well and what could be improved. Critically, it should drive out learnings and actions to improve your future crisis response, or, even better, to prevent the next crisis happening at all (see Chapter 15).

Supporting materials

Supporting materials are the resources that enable your crisis management team to do its job quickly and efficiently. They are designed to save time, aid prioritisation and avoid oversights, and include:

- **Resources** such as site plans, maps of surrounding areas and relevant company policies

- **Forms and templates** such as action and decision logs, information gathering checklists, briefing notes for receptionists and security staff

- **'How to' guides** such as how to initiate a videoconference, how to set up the crisis team room, how and where to access files and documents

- **Contact details for:**
  - The crisis management team
  - Other colleagues who may require communication

- Stakeholders such as customers, investors and regulators
- Business partners and suppliers

These materials should be cross referenced in team members' action checklists so they are easily accessible when required.

Communication

Effective communication is fundamental to retaining the trust and confidence of your stakeholders in a crisis. It is, therefore, an essential element of crisis management planning.

More than that, your communication must be rooted in your overall crisis management strategy and synchronised with your operational response. As a consequence, many organisations include crisis communication as part of their crisis management plan, while others develop a separate but complementary crisis communication plan.

So long as communication is a fully integrated element of your overall crisis response (not a bolt on, separate function or afterthought) either approach is valid. For the purposes of this book, I have assumed that you are developing a separate crisis communication plan, and this is described in Chapter 9. Whichever route you take, the fundamental purpose, structure and strategic importance of your crisis communication plan remain the same.

Summary

A crisis management plan does not in and of itself guarantee you will respond effectively to a breaking situation. Nor will it provide all the answers and it certainly won't make decisions for you.

It will ensure a purposeful, well-organised way of working and provide critical resources to enable you to get on top of a situation quickly.

Questions

- Have you been involved in responding to a crisis? What role did your crisis management plan play in responding to it? If there was no plan, what happened as a result?

- Do you have an existing crisis management plan? If so, how does it compare with the structure and content outlined here? What's missing? When was it last updated?

- Do you/will you include communication in your crisis management plan or as a separate document?

NINE

How To Develop Your Crisis Communication Plan

'It takes many good deeds to build a good reputation, and only one bad one to lose it.'
— Benjamin Franklin

A crisis brings unprecedented stakeholder attention demanding immediate answers, information and reassurance. The list of interested parties seems endless: customers, the media, investors, regulators, emergency services, officials, employees, neighbours, pressure groups, politicians and more.

Protecting your business in the wake of a major incident requires you to fix the problem at the heart of your crisis. However, on its own this is not enough to guarantee a successful outcome. That requires problem resolution *and* simultaneous communication. One without the other is never enough.

Indeed, how effectively you communicate with your stakeholders in a crisis is often the determining factor in the overall success of your crisis management.

A crisis tests your PR team like nothing else; if you are not geared up for this challenge, reputational damage is almost inevitable.

The role of communication in crisis management

Oxford Metrica's studies have demonstrated that the way in which a business responds to a crisis defines the extent to which value is lost (or sometimes won). They call it the 'acid test' of management.

Its 2011 Reputation Review, produced in partnership with AON's risk management practice, includes valuable insights, especially the impact of crisis communication on value recovery or loss. Oxford Metrica concluded that the quality of communication had a direct effect on the financial impact on the business.

In particular, those that retained or grew their value after an incident:

- Disclosed information promptly

- Demonstrated candour and transparency in their disclosure

- Took responsibility for their actions (or those of their agents)

- Demonstrated credible follow-up behaviours

Those that lost the most value:

- Either delayed communication or failed to communicate at all

- Issued opaque or partial responses

- Failed to take responsibility or express contrition

- Attempted to shift blame

These are well-known golden rules of successful crisis communication so why do so many organisations fail to adhere to them when crisis strikes? Stagecoach's Steven Stewart explains: 'Leaders sometimes worry they may say the wrong thing and as a consequence decide not to say anything at all.'

Communicating in a crisis is extremely uncomfortable and seizing the initiative requires courage. Experience shows that honest, open, early and frequent communication is the only way to ensure that reputational value is protected rather than eroded.

One of the best illustrations of the benefits of a proactive communication approach is the response of Norsk Hydro, one of the world's largest aluminium companies, to a major ransomware attack in March 2019.

As soon as the severity of the situation became apparent, the management team held an urgent meeting during which they made two key decisions to underpin their response: they would not pay the ransom and they would be completely open about the attack.

By committing to communicating transparently and frequently from the outset, Norsk Hydro set themselves on the right course to retain the trust of their stakeholders. At the same time, they were living by their values given that, according to Halvor Molland, senior vice president of media relations, transparency is core to Norsk Hydro's culture.

The consistent flow of information from the company delivered via various communication channels – including regular media statements, daily press conferences, social media posts and journalist open days – gave the outside world confidence that Norsk Hydro was taking control of the situation.

Employees received regular updates, sometimes via creative means. During the early phase of the crisis, when electronic communication was impossible, executives used handwritten notes and signs posted around entrances, stairwells and elevators to tell employees not to connect devices to the company network.

Norsk Hydro's open communication approach paid dividends. According to Inger Sethov, Norsk Hydro's head of communications and public affairs, 'External stakeholders appreciated the transparency and openness ... the share price went up!'

Protecting your reputation will always be a top priority in a crisis and to do so you must communicate well. No crisis can be successfully resolved if either the communication *or* the operational response is ineffective.

The purpose of a crisis communication plan

A crisis communication plan provides the foundation from which to protect your reputation. It should enable you to communicate quickly and appropriately with stakeholders to retain their trust and protect your reputation. Through a combination of clear ways of working, checklists, templated communication materials and helpful resources it is designed to give your communication team the ability to exert influence over the situation at the earliest opportunity.

An effective crisis communication plan ensures your stakeholders receive clear, timely, consistent information while your operational team grapples with the crisis itself.

Essential content

As suggested in Chapter 8, for the purposes of this book we will assume that your crisis management and crisis communication plans are two separate documents. The same principles apply if your crisis communication plan is included within your crisis management plan as an appendix.

Your crisis communication plan must align and integrate with your crisis management plan and include the following.

Purpose and scope of the plan

A description of what the plan covers and its role. Critically, it should articulate the difference between this plan and your crisis management plan and how they interrelate with each other.

Roles and responsibilities

A crisis affects multiple stakeholders and therefore multiple roles are required to interact with them. These could cover:

- Media relations

- Social media

- Internal communication

- Investor relations

- Government relations

You may also choose to create task-related roles, for example:

- **Message development:** creating the message themes that must underpin and be consistent across all communication and stakeholder groups

- **Content development:** drafting statements, briefings, social media posts, website content and so on

- **Media monitoring:** tracking and analysing coverage about the crisis on traditional, online and social media

Include a short summary of the scope and purpose of each role in your crisis communication plan. If you do not have a sufficiently large communication team to assign a different person to each role, individuals may need to cover multiple roles. Alternatively, you could call in third parties such as your PR agency to expand your team.

First actions checklist

A list of the critical actions that must be completed by the crisis communication team during the first hour of a crisis (the 'golden hour') will enable you to prioritise the most important tasks and thereby begin to influence the narrative at the earliest opportunity.

Checklist of tasks for individual team roles

A role-by-role checklist of key tasks provides clarity and focus for team members.

Key communication principles

This will include, for example, your crisis communication objectives and in principle message formulas.

Guidelines to help shape your communication response

These could include, for example:

- Decision-making criteria to help determine whether to communicate proactively or reactively

- Criteria to guide whether a press conference is appropriate or not

Forms and logs to manage stakeholder interaction

These may include:

- A stakeholder communication plan framework setting out what must be communicated to whom, by when and through which channel (email, the media, phone call, face-to-face briefing, etc)

- A media enquiry log

- A stakeholder enquiry log

Template communication materials

Having ready-made materials to hand can save a critical thirty minutes when you need them most, so develop the following template communication materials against your key risks with space to fill in details about the precise situation:

- Media statements

- Internal briefings

- Customer briefings

- Social media posts

Have these statements pre-approved (especially by your legal team) to reduce the turn-around time in a live situation.

'How to' guides

Draft step-by-step guidelines for some of the critical tasks required to enact your communication response. For example:

- How to upload material to your website

- How to activate social media monitoring

- How to set up a video conference

Make sure they are drafted in such a way that they could be applied by someone who had never seen them before. As Cathay Pacific's Gus Whitcomb says:

> 'We're very good at stating what we need to do, but not so good at articulating how we're going to do it. For example, our checklist might say "distribute the media statement", but that's just the "what". If you think about "how", who is going to do that? Who's their backup? What list are they going to use? Where's that located? Are we going to do this by email, by SMS, by fax? What account are we going to use? Who has the pass codes? Who checks to see if there are any bounce backs and what should we do if there are?'

Team contact details

Include contact details, not just for your internal team members, but for anyone who might be part of your extended communication team, for example:

- Your PR agency
- Your media monitoring agency
- Your social media monitoring company
- Your advertising agency
- Your social media agency
- Your website designer

Stakeholder lists

Include contact details for all stakeholders with whom you may need to communicate in a crisis. Consider pre-defining in principle priority levels for stakeholders. Guy Esnouf, who has held senior communication positions at businesses including npower, Microsoft and GSK, suggests: 'Focus first on your employees. You cannot run a business without the confidence of your employees. Secondly, customers. If you get those two right, everything else will take care of itself.'

Approval process

Agree a streamlined approval process in advance of a crisis, one which will enable approval of communication materials in no more than thirty minutes. This will likely be different to your business-as-usual approval process and require fewer people to be involved in the process. As Guy Esnouf says: 'A lack of speed kills communication activities in a crisis and the most common challenge, in my experience, is that you can't get an approval. Get your approval routes sorted out before you need to make a statement.'

Summary

For your business to emerge successfully from a crisis requires it to fix the underlying issue and communicate with its stakeholders simultaneously.

Well-judged, timely communication is essential to set the narrative, retain the trust and confidence of your stakeholders and protect your reputation.

Your crisis communication plan provides the framework to meet this challenge.

Questions

- With which stakeholder groups might you need to communicate in a crisis?

- Which risks require template communication materials?

- Who are the most important stakeholder groups against these risks?

- Who should be included in your extended communication team?

- Who would need to approve your communication materials in a crisis? How quickly could you secure their approval?

SECTION FOUR
TRAIN

TEN

Creating An Effective Crisis Management Team

> 'It's next to impossible to construct a team in the heat of a crisis. You want to go through that process way in advance. It's about identifying the right people – and they aren't always the most senior people.'
> — Steven Stewart, Director of Communications, Stagecoach Group

Plans provide an invaluable framework for managing a crisis, but people are even more important. Under pressure, the people on your crisis management team (CMT) are required to assess the situation, set a clear strategy, make critical decisions, develop and execute your action plan and communicate with your stakeholders in such a way that it retains their trust and confidence.

The make-up of your team should address the unique dynamics of a crisis rather than reflecting business as usual.

As Jim French from Lundin Mining explains: 'A crisis management structure is different from the traditional hierarchical structure of the organisation because it's based on the skillsets of the individuals, and the crisis management roles they are assigned.'

A crisis calls for a range of capabilities: planning, decision-making, project management, communication, analysis, creativity. As a consequence, your team should include a diverse set of personality types and individual strengths. It should feature introverts and extroverts. Charismatic leaders and reflective thinkers. Optimists and pessimists.

Avoid at all costs a team dominated by individuals who share a similar personality type. This can result in 'groupthink' and leave you without the broad range of skills and attributes that are essential to overcome a crisis. Select the right people, not just the most senior.

This chapter explains the roles that should be represented on your CMT and the responsibilities associated with each one. It also provides guidance on the personal qualities and characteristics that must be present in your team.

The role of your crisis management team

Your CMT is the body of people responsible for guiding your business through its worst nightmares. At a strategic level, the team sets direction, makes critical decisions and provides support for those in the front line. It also plays a key role in communication.

As Lidl's Katrin Suesser says:

> 'A clear crisis management team structure is very important. If everyone understands what they have to do (and also what other members of the team must do), it's so much easier. Clear roles and responsibilities are essential for the team to work effectively.'

To make swift, purposeful progress in a crisis, your team should comprise the minimum number of people with the necessary knowledge and skills required to effectively manage the situation.

Having too many people in the room unnecessarily prolongs discussion and diverts resources from managing the crisis itself. Having too few people risks a lack of informed contributions or challenge, resulting in 'groupthink'. A core group of six to eight people is usually about right.

Successfully managing a crisis demands many different skills and requires a wide range of tasks to be completed. Your team should include a diverse range of people in terms of their professional expertise, experience, capabilities and personality types.

Do *not* pre-assign a single, specified individual to a particular role on your team. This creates a single point of failure if that person is unavailable on the day the crisis breaks, so ensure that every role has at least one deputy. With a well-drilled team, a single person will be capable of playing one of several potential roles.

Focus not on the people but instead on the roles, responsibilities and tasks associated with each. List in your plan two or more candidates for each role. When the crisis occurs, confirm one of them in position.

CMT roles fall into two different categories: **core roles** and **specialist roles**.

Core roles

Core roles are required within *every* CMT, either to ensure the crisis management process functions efficiently, or because their area of expertise (for example legal, HR or communication) is relevant to every incident type.

These core roles typically include the following.

Team leader

This person is responsible for chairing the CMT, strategy and decision-making during a crisis. Given its strategic focus and ultimate decision-making power, it is most often played by your CEO, managing director or COO.

As Sky's Eilish McGuinness explains:

> 'It must be someone who has the respect of their team and is comfortable making quick decisions. They need to be able to say: "We have ten minutes to discuss this critical issue but then we're making a decision and moving on." This is not a collaborative thing. It's command and control.'

The following personality traits, capabilities and characteristics are desirable in the role of team leader:

- Commands the respect of the team
- Ability to see the bigger picture
- Ability to focus on the long term
- Courage to make difficult decisions in a timely manner
- Influencing skills
- Listening skills

- Well organised and purposeful

- Has emotional intelligence

- Possesses good judgement

- Willing and able to delegate

- Ability to remain calm

- Resilient and emotionally robust

- Media handling skills (in the event that they act as spokesperson)

Crisis coordinator

The crisis coordinator is the first lieutenant to the CMT leader. They ensure that the crisis management plan and processes are followed and all necessary logistical and administrative support is provided. Given the need to be fully conversant with the organisation's crisis management plans and processes, this role is often played by the person responsible for the overall crisis management programme.

An effective crisis coordinator will possess the following characteristics:

- Respected and trusted by those on the CMT (especially the leader)

- Strong organisational skills

- Excellent project management skills

- Systematic and well organised

- Self-confident

- Influencing skills

- Conscientious/diligent

- Methodical

- Calm under pressure

Administrator(s)

Crisis administrators record key decisions and actions and provide whatever other administrative support is required by the CMT. Do not underestimate the importance of the administrator role. They are not only critical to the effective running of the CMT during an incident, the record they keep will be of vital importance in any subsequent review or investigation.

The ability to log accurate information and record decisions and actions while a CMT meeting is in session is not an easy task. This is why having a team of two administrators working alongside each other is highly beneficial.

Administrators should possess the following personal qualities:

- Attention to detail/accuracy

- Ability to work at pace under pressure

- Willing to challenge/correct/check information with senior team members

- Unflappable

- Self-confident

- Good listener

- Resilient

Information lead

The information lead gathers and updates facts, which are displayed on a (physical or online) situation overview board throughout the crisis. It is their role to ensure that the entire team has easy access to the latest confirmed information about the crisis.

Your information lead should display the following characteristics:

- Analytical skills

- Able to evaluate information in terms of quality and relevance

- Can filter, analyse and make sense of information

- Able to present information to decision makers clearly and succinctly

- Calm under pressure

- Thoughtful

- Well organised

- Good communicator

Legal lead

Your legal lead advises on legal implications of the situation and the risks associated with alternative courses of action. The role would typically be played by your general counsel, in-house lawyer or external legal advisor.

It is important that your legal and communication leads build relationships and agree ways of working ahead of a crisis. Failing to do this risks heated discussions or disagreements at a time when alignment is essential.

As Stagecoach's Steven Stewart observes:

'Both parties must value each other's input, so make sure you understand where your counterpart is coming from. Recognise your views are equally valid: they are just different parts of a process that goes into reaching decisions. One is not better, or more right, than the other.'

Communication lead

The communication lead advises the CMT on the reputational impact of the crisis and directs communication strategy. Effective stakeholder communication is essential if you are to maintain their trust and confidence in a crisis and for this reason the communication role is a critical one.

Given that the communication lead's primary responsibility is to advise the CMT, ideally they should not also be personally responsible for the drafting of communication materials or handling media calls. They require a team or PR agency to undertake these tasks.

As NFU Mutual's Jo Lumani says, the communication lead must give their best advice, however uncomfortable it may be:

> 'There are times in a crisis when your advice may be the antithesis of what the chief executive wants to hear. Nevertheless, you should always voice concern when you believe it is in the best interests of the business. Be courageous in challenging your leadership team but do it with respect, insight and gravitas rather than shouting and stamping your feet.'

The communication lead should display the following characteristics:

- Understands media and other stakeholders' communication needs
- Empathy: can see stakeholders' points of view
- Willing to challenge expedient decisions; comfortable playing the role of 'devil's advocate'
- Ability to see the long-term reputational implications of decisions
- Trusted and respected by the senior team
- Good listener
- Influencing skills
- Self-confident
- Media handling skills

HR lead

Your HR lead is responsible for advising on the employee aspects of the crisis. This can include everything from internal communication to trauma counselling and disciplinary procedures in the event of serious misconduct. They will often work closely with the communication and legal leads. Given that almost every crisis has some form of impact on your people, the role of HR lead is very important.

Spokesperson

Your spokesperson undertakes media interviews and relevant stakeholder briefings on your behalf. In the event of an extended crisis they will become the face and voice of the organisation, so selecting the right person for this role is of critical importance. Make the judgement of who should be your spokesperson on a crisis-by-crisis basis dependent upon the magnitude and nature of the situation.

When making your decision, the right job title is important, but it is nowhere near as important as the ability to represent the organisation in the best possible way under pressure. This requires advanced communication skills, empathy, emotional intelligence and a cool head.

Determining whether to field your CEO for media interviews is a big decision. Doing so demonstrates responsibility and shows that the organisation is treating the situation with the utmost seriousness and cares deeply about what has happened.

However, once your CEO becomes your media spokesperson it can be extremely hard for them to extricate themselves from this role, as BP's Tony Hayward discovered to his cost. The role of spokesperson can become all-consuming, preventing your CEO from fulfilling any other role on the CMT or focusing on their day job. For this reason, deploy your CEO as spokesperson only in the most serious of circumstances and ensure you have an experienced deputy to step into their role as team leader.

Scenario planners

In Chapter 7, I described how scenario planning can help businesses prepare for high-risk situations as part of pre-crisis planning. It has an equally important role during a crisis.

Scenario planners consider worst-case scenarios and brainstorm how the situation may develop over the coming days and weeks. To achieve breadth of thinking, it is helpful to have at least two scenario planners working on this task.

To be effective in identifying where the crisis could go to next and how it could become even more challenging, they require a quiet place to think and work. Therefore, they will sit outside of the CMT for the large part but will join them periodically to share their views of the future for consideration by the team.

Necessary qualities and capabilities for this role include:

- Creative
- Open-minded
- Ability to look at a situation from multiple perspectives

- Innovative
- Knowledgeable, experienced and worldly
- Challenging/contrary
- Thoughtful
- Reflective
- Far-sighted
- Respected by the team

Devil's advocate

The devil's advocate is tasked with taking an 'outside in' perspective, sense-checking actions and challenging decisions. While the role is not mandatory, it can be a valuable antidote to groupthink and cognitive dissonance.

The ability to put yourself in the shoes of your stakeholders is an essential requirement for a devil's advocate, which is why communication professionals are well suited to this role.

Characteristics of an effective devil's advocate include:

- Empathy: can see stakeholders' point of view
- Challenging/contrary
- Independent thinker

- Deep understanding of and passion for your brand

- Self-confident

- Respected by the team

Specialist roles and experts

In addition to core CMT roles to be filled whatever the crisis type, you also require specialists who are assigned to your team based on the nature of the crisis and their specific expertise. They bring specialist knowledge required to address a particular crisis type.

For example, in a cyber crisis it would be your chief information security officer. In the event of a product contamination, it could be your head of production or quality.

Specialist roles will differ from business to business, but can include:

- **IT/IS/technology:** advising on the IT impact of a crisis, especially in the event of a cyber incident.

- **Health, safety and the environment:** advising on the health and safety implications of an accident or other incident that could harm people or the environment.

- **Finance:** advising on the financial impact of a crisis, investor relations and liaison with insurers. Especially relevant to crises such as allegations of fraud or false accounting.

- **Operations:** advising on the operational impacts of a crisis and how it may affect the normal running of the business. This is of particular importance if the crisis relates to manufacturing, production or supply chain management.

- **Sales:** advising on the commercial impact of a crisis, especially where customer relationships may be affected.

- **Marketing:** advising on the brand impact of a crisis, especially when the crisis relates to marketing activity such as an advertising campaign or celebrity endorsement.

- **Business unit heads:** co-opted onto the CMT to provide an informed perspective if the crisis affects their part of the business.

- **Country/regional heads:** co-opted onto the CMT to provide an 'on the ground' perspective if the crisis affects their part of the world.

This is not an exhaustive list. Consider what specialist roles might be required for your business given its operations and risk profile.

Your extended crisis management team

Crises are extraordinary events that place an unprecedented demand on your internal resources. Do not underestimate the challenge this presents: your business-as-usual team and resources will be stretched to the limit (and sometimes beyond).

It is therefore inevitable that you will require external support to add brains, arms and legs to your in-house team when a crisis occurs.

Plan for this ahead of the event: avoid at all costs the need to identify, screen and appoint legal advisors, cyber experts, forensic accountants or communication advisors when the crisis is raging around you.

As Stagecoach's Steven Stewart points out:

> 'You need partners that really understand your business, not just its operations, but also its culture. If your consultancy partner doesn't understand the personality of your organisation and how it operates, they will be unable to develop the most effective approach to prepare your business for a crisis. The best consultancies get under the skin of an organisation before beginning crisis planning. They understand that so much of a company's response to a crisis depends on its culture.'

In Chapter 3, we set out a list of providers of expertise and resources you might need in a crisis. Revisit this list and identify what types of support your business may require. Where you have existing relationships, brief them on what you expect from them in a crisis and confirm they are able to provide it. Where gaps remain, identify and put on standby new partners.

Agree the basis on which you are retaining their services and add their contact details to your crisis management plan. If they are critical partners (for example, your PR agency) involve them in briefings, drills and exercises.

If you are unable to meet the demands of a crisis with the right quantity and quality of resource, you will quickly lose control of it. Invest time ahead of an incident to identify, appoint and build relationships with critical partners.

Summary

The quality of your CMT and its ability to operate effectively under extreme pressure with high stakes will dictate the success of your crisis response.

Ensure the core roles on your team are well understood and that every potential role holder has at least one nominated deputy who has been briefed and trained.

Identify internal subject matter experts whose deep knowledge will be required, dependent upon the crisis type.

Build up a network of external partners to provide advice and guidance in a crisis, along with providers of additional resource so you can scale up your team when you need it most.

Questions

- Who are the candidates for core roles on your CMT?

- Which internal specialists or experts might you need to assign to the crisis team dependent upon the crisis type?

- What personal strengths and personality types are represented on your team? What characteristics are lacking?

- What kind of external advisors or experts might you need? Which do you already have in place? What are you currently lacking from your roster?

ELEVEN

How To Develop A Highly Effective Crisis Management Team

'You can't expect people to succeed without training: they must be confident of their own personal skillset and understand how they operate as part of a team.'
— Mark Wenham, former head of the Defence Media Operations Centre

A crisis breaks. The team assembles. The carefully created crisis management plan is about to be put to the test. It contains everything the team needs to guide their crisis response: principles, guidelines, checklists, resources and templated materials.

Why is it that, all too often, plans are given only a cursory glance at the beginning of an incident or, worse, remain unopened on the table?

In the best-case scenario, it is because team members are so well trained and drilled on the plan they have developed 'muscle memory' and the plan is already embedded in their consciousness. This is the mark of a truly effective CMT.

Sadly, there is another less positive reason why teams fail to refer to their crisis management plan: they have never been trained on it or, in some cases, even read it.

As Mark Wenham says: 'If you immerse someone in an intense pressure situation without training, they are almost guaranteed to fail.'

Having invested time to prepare a crisis management plan to support the business in its hour of need, you must ensure team members have the knowledge, understanding and confidence to apply it. That process begins with briefing and training, and concludes with exercising, more of which in Chapters 12 and 13.

How to brief your crisis management team

Developing your crisis management plan is a critical first step in crisis management, but it is of limited value unless your people are familiar with it. A perfect plan is of no use unless it is embedded within the organisation.

Everyone, from your chief executive through to your call centre operators and the administrators logging actions and decisions, has an important role to play and they all need to know what is expected of them.

While circulating your plan to CMT members is a good start, it is insufficient to build the knowledge, understanding and confidence required to deploy it.

The process of building confidence in a plan truly begins with a structured team briefing workshop. During this session, team members should be walked through the plan and given a first opportunity to practise applying key elements of it through interactive exercises and discussion.

In addition to a briefing on plan structure, content and principles, they should be introduced to key processes: the aim is not to test them, but to familiarise them with the plan.

By the end of the workshop your team members should understand:

- The definition of a crisis for your business

- Your objectives and principles for crisis management

- How the CMT is activated

- How the CMT is structured, its roles and responsibilities, candidates for key roles and their deputies

- The standing agenda for CMT meetings

- The importance of 'strategic intent' in a crisis, what it is and how to develop it

- How to develop your crisis response plan

- How situation updates, decisions and actions will be recorded

- The structure and format for your stakeholder engagement plan

- Actions to be completed in the first hour and by whom

At the end of the plan briefing (typically two to three hours in length) your team will have a much clearer understanding of what the crisis management plan contains and their role within it. Make sure there's time for questions and check in with your colleagues a few days later to identify any issues arising.

A plan briefing is the critical first step in ensuring your crisis management plan will be executed effectively should the worst occur.

How to train your crisis management team

It's optimistic at best to expect people to successfully fulfil any new role without experience and training. To imagine they can do so in a crisis, when the stakes are high and pressure is intense, is foolhardy in the extreme.

Even if members of your team are naturally skilled in decision-making, communication, information management or situational awareness, crisis management is a team game and they need to understand how their contribution fits into the overall team effort.

The bottom line is that you will only succeed in protecting your business and its reputation if everyone involved in crisis response understands their role and responsibilities.

Each of the roles within your CMT requires different skills and capabilities: one size does *not* fit all when it comes to crisis management. Role-specific training is therefore the best way of giving CMT members the knowledge, skills and confidence to play their part in a successful response.

As Kim Green, a writer and pilot, observes:

> 'If you've never handled a major emergency, it's hard to know how you'll fare when your

first one hits. That's why pilots are trained in crisis management. We're taught to think through a range of potential mishaps, memorise checklists, and plot courses of action in advance. Executives can do the same.'

In addition to an in-depth briefing on the specific tasks associated with a person's likely role on the team, consider capability-building in the following areas.

Crisis management team leader

- Strategy development

- Decision-making

- Meeting management

- Listening skills

- Emotional intelligence

- Team management

- Influencing skills

- Communication skills

- Delegation and empowerment

Crisis management coordinator

- Project management

- Planning skills

- Influencing skills
- Communication skills

Spokesperson

- Communication skills
- Understanding the media agenda
- Effective interview preparation
- Delivering key messages
- Tone and body language
- Dealing with challenging questions

Scenario planner

- Scenario planning techniques
- Creative thinking

Administrator

- Staying calm under pressure
- Personal impact/communication skills
- Active listening
- Assertiveness

In addition to members of your CMT, consider training other staff members likely to be involved in crisis response. Pay particular attention to people in the frontline who may be approached by stakeholders for information about the crisis. They can include receptionists, call centre operators, security guards, salespeople and switchboard operators.

For these people, schedule a training workshop covering:

- The value of your business's reputation and your role in protecting it
- What to do and who to call if you become aware of a potential incident
- An introduction to the media
- Dealing with media enquiries – tips, techniques and tools
- Dealing with other stakeholders

Role-specific training for team members ensures everyone is ready to play their part in protecting your business in the event of a crisis. Make sure that deputies are included in the training to ensure strength in depth.

Finally, never think that your training programme is complete. As Lidl's Aoife Clarke says:

'Crisis management is not a project with a start and end date. It's something the business is fully invested in for the long term and we keep it in our mind all the time. We understand it's not enough to do one crisis simulation and think "that's it, we're trained".'

Make sure that new starters are inducted into your CMT and keep skills fresh with refresher training, for example by inviting a guest speaker to talk about their experiences of crisis management or running a 'lunch and learn' session to discuss a recent crisis from your sector (more on this in Chapter 15 on continuous improvement).

Summary

Developing a crisis management plan is a critical first step in crisis management, but it means nothing unless people know that it exists and what it contains. Running a plan briefing gives your team members a foundation of understanding that underpins a successful crisis response.

Individuals expected to take on roles within your CMT must be briefed on what is expected of them, trained on their essential tasks and coached on the softer skills required in their role.

Providing this level of training significantly increases the likelihood of your plan being deployed effectively under pressure.

Questions

- Who needs to be briefed on your crisis management plan?

- In addition to being briefed, what additional training would team members benefit from to help them play their role more effectively?

- Who are the 'frontliners' in your organisation? What training do they require?

SECTION FIVE
EXERCISE

TWELVE

Why Exercise?

'Success has to do with deliberate practice.
Practice must be focused, determined, and in an
environment where there's feedback.'
— Malcolm Gladwell

A crisis is a defining moment in an organisation's history: making the right decisions at that time determines your fate. The likelihood of making the right calls under enormous pressure is much higher for businesses that have properly rehearsed their crisis response beforehand.

Just like any other task, practice makes perfect. A programme of crisis exercising builds confidence and capability, resulting in a well-drilled team able to deliver a pitch-perfect response under an intense spotlight.

Failing to regularly rehearse leaves you seriously exposed in the event of a crisis. A CMT with a plan but without an exercise is like giving an orchestra a musical score but no rehearsal and expecting them to perform flawlessly on a concert hall stage.

As Sky's Eilish McGuinness points out:

> 'There's a temptation to just plan and plan and plan, believing that a fancy plan will protect your business if a crisis strikes. Unfortunately, you rarely have a detailed plan ready for whatever the exact scenario turns out to be. So, you have to exercise as well. How do you know what good looks like? You have to see it. How do you know what bad looks like? You have to see it. Don't wait until you think your plan is perfect before exercising. Do it now. You will discover some amazing capabilities within your team and also some areas you need to work on.'

The purpose of exercising

Rick Rescorla was Head of Security at Morgan Stanley, which was based at the World Trade Center in New York. Morgan Stanley occupied twenty-two floors of the South Tower.

Rescorla had long been concerned about the World Trade Center being a possible terrorist target. Prior to the 1993 World Trade Center bombing, he and one of his associates, Daniel Hill, had identified the basement of the building as being an easy target for terrorist activity.

After sadly being proved right by the events of 1993 and being dissatisfied with how the first responders handled the evacuation, Rescorla vowed to make changes. He believed the World Trade Center continued to represent a significant terrorist threat – particularly from the air – and recommended that Morgan Stanley vacate the premises. However, due to lease obligations, that was not a viable option.

Instead, Rescorla developed a rigorous emergency evacuation plan and was scrupulous about regular exercising. He ran drills every three months – sometimes to the dismay of employees keen to avoid work interruptions – to ensure everyone knew how to escape the tower in the minimum amount of time.

On that fateful day in 2001 when the first plane struck the North Tower, Rescorla immediately activated his evacuation plan, ignoring an intercom announcement instructing people to stay in the building.

Due to the regular training they had received, every employee knew exactly what they had to do. One survivor, David Ricca, said of the training:

'All his [Rescorla's] teachings and all his drills really made an impact. Some people didn't like being interrupted in business hours but I'm so glad that he did it. To teach us what needed to be done because it [the death toll] could have been so much worse.'

As a result, just thirteen Morgan Stanley workers (including, sadly, Rick Rescorla himself) out of the near 2,700-strong workforce died in the attacks, despite having to evacuate from some of the highest floors in the tower. Without that rehearsal, it could have been a different story for the employees at Morgan Stanley.

Exercising builds muscle memory. By practising ways of working in a crisis, a team becomes comfortable working under pressure. They understand what needs to be done, when and how. This creates confidence and assurance, which is lacking in teams who fail to rehearse. It means the team can focus on the really important parts of managing the crisis – making big decisions – rather than worrying about the process itself.

Ultimately, this is the purpose of exercising: developing a capable, confident team that instinctively knows what to do when a crisis breaks. More than that, exercising demonstrates to your people that you genuinely care about their safety and wellbeing and underlines your commitment to being a responsible business.

The value of exercising is ingrained within astronauts, who may need to make life and death decisions under the gravest of circumstances. Take NASA's Commander Chris Hadfield, for example.

During the BBC television series *Astronauts: Do you have what it takes?*, he recounted the story of his first space flight when he had the task of docking the Space Shuttle with the Russian space station MIR. It's a complex and challenging manoeuvre at the best of times, so you can imagine the pressure when, with just 10 metres to go, all systems failed. Despite this, the manoeuvre was completed perfectly.

Why? Because, according to Commander Hadfield, 'We'd practised like crazy on every simulator you can think of; our success under enormous pressure was a result of relentless practising for when things go wrong.'

That's why exercising for crisis situations is so important, whether or not you're an astronaut.

In addition to building mental 'muscle memory', exercising delivers broader benefits. Firstly, you will identify flaws in your plan, deficiencies in your capability and resource gaps. All of these can be addressed, but without an exercise they will lie undetected only to become apparent when a crisis strikes.

Secondly, personality types and team dynamics emerge during exercising. Prior knowledge of these dynamics is invaluable in the event of a live crisis; it may even persuade you to change the make-up of your team. As NFU Mutual's Jo Lumani observes:

'Exercising is the most useful way of identifying how people operate under pressure. It may change how you deploy them in a real situation. Some people are built for crisis and others are uncomfortable with it. Exercising enables you to look at strengths and development areas of your team members. People who hide their light under a bushel on a day-to-day basis may come to the fore in an exercise. Equally, you may find that someone you had expected to play a key role is not at all comfortable in those situations. It's better to identify that during an exercise than a live incident.'

Thirdly, a rehearsal makes your whole organisation much more vigilant and crisis-aware, reducing the likelihood of a crisis.

Finally, exercising also has benefits in terms of business as usual. Skills learned and rehearsed during an exercise – decision-making under pressure, communication and teamwork, for example – are all capabilities that are valuable not just in a crisis but also on a day-to-day basis.

Different exercise types and the benefits of each

Exercises come in many shapes and sizes so it's important to understand and select the right type at the right time.

This begins with setting clear objectives. Ask yourself: why are we doing this exercise? What are we seeking to achieve? What outcomes do we want to get out of this?

NFU Mutual's Jo Lumani is an advocate for this approach. She advises:

> 'Have very clear expectations for any exercise. It's about knowing the capabilities of your team and setting the pace of the exercise accordingly. There are times to put people under pressure and there are times when our aim is to get people acquainted with the plan and familiar with their roles. If you've got a very inexperienced team and you put them through the worst day of their lives, they will just completely disengage and won't want to be involved in anything in the future.'

Is the main aim of the exercise to build your team's confidence in a new plan? To develop your response to an emerging risk such as cyber attacks? Or maybe test the performance of your team under extreme pressure? Your objective will affect your choice of exercise type.

You should also pay close attention to the experience level of your team when determining the format for your exercise. Drop an inexperienced CMT straight into an immersive simulation and failure is all but guaranteed. Scenario planning workshops, crisis management plan briefings and desktop exercises should all be considered ahead of a full simulation.

Understanding precisely why you are doing a simulation and what you want to achieve, as well as the experience level of your team, will help you select the correct format from the range of exercises outlined below.

As Lundin Mining's Jim French observes:

> 'Exercises need to be realistic, but it's important to calibrate the level of pressure presented based on the maturity of the team. There must be a level of stress in your exercises, which I refer to as "healthy tension". Exercises also need to be paced since they are learning sessions. It's a very fine balance. Most importantly though, it's critical not to overwhelm people and to be alert for signs of unhealthy stress and fatigue.'

Drills

A drill is the most basic type of crisis exercise, usually rehearsing the initial communication and activation process. For example, it may involve sending SMS messages to CMT members to check they are received and responded to.

Drills may also require the CMT to form (either virtually or remotely) to test how quickly and efficiently the team can be activated. This kind of drill can also include setting up the logistics and technology in the crisis team room.

Drills take little time to prepare and last no longer than ninety minutes (often less), so consider running them every quarter.

As Cathay Pacific's Gus Whitcomb explains: 'We do walkthroughs of basic processes that we want to make sure are working properly. We'll get everybody who's involved together and take it from A to Z to make sure all the pieces fit together.'

Drills are important because, until the team is up and working, your business is unable to exert any influence over the escalating situation. Ensuring these initial steps are ingrained in team members and confirming you can get to work quickly with minimum fuss is therefore an essential part of your crisis exercising.

Desktop exercise

Facilitated 'desktop exercises' are an important part of an ongoing crisis management exercising programme, especially when you want to embed a new crisis management plan or rehearse a new or inexperienced team.

They are based on a realistic scenario against which your crisis management plan is applied and take place in a physical or online meeting room.

During the exercise, regular inputs – status updates, emails, social media screengrabs and previously prepared radio news broadcasts – are fed into your team by a facilitator to pose new challenges and test its capabilities.

Your team must determine its crisis management strategy, make decisions, develop its action plan and determine communication tactics in response to unfolding events. Crucially, though, a desktop exercise does not require role players and while the team discusses and confirms its response to each stage of the scenario, they do not enact it.

The team's decisions are probed and challenged by the facilitator who will adjust pressure according to how they are performing. The session concludes with a debrief, discussion of learnings and commitment to actions.

A desktop exercise increases the knowledge, capability and confidence of your team to respond effectively to a crisis. It also tests your plans and processes to identify where there are gaps, flawed processes or missing resources.

Depending on your risk profile and appetite for crisis exercising, run at least one desktop exercise every year.

Crisis simulation

Anyone who has experienced a crisis understands that its unique pressure calls for ways of working far removed from business as usual.

A full crisis simulation gives you reassurance that your plan works under fire or identifies areas that require further work. It will also verify which team members are capable of fulfilling their roles and responsibilities under stress in a crisis and who needs further training. In some cases, you will discover that the skillset of certain individuals means they should not be part of your CMT.

Crisis simulations immerse your team in a realistic crisis scenario, receiving calls and emails from a host of role players representing colleagues, investors, customers, regulators and media. As well as setting strategy, decision-making and action planning, your team must deal with social media and conduct media interviews.

A simulation requires meticulous preparation if you are to create a realistic yet challenging scenario that demands the attention of your team (see Chapter 13 for how to develop a scenario that meets these criteria).

At the conclusion of any exercise you should run a structured debrief on your crisis response and discuss where improvements can be made. If a third party is running the exercise, ask them to produce a post-exercise report assessing your capabilities and outlining next steps.

Until you participate in a crisis simulation you cannot know whether or not your team will rise to the unique challenge of a crisis and successfully protect your business and its reputation. Completing a simulation gives you capability and confidence to be sure you can. As such, a full simulation should be completed on an annual basis.

War gaming

As the name suggests, war gaming is based on a methodology originally deployed by the military when planning its interaction with an adversary.

Former British Army officer Mark Wenham explains:

'War gaming or red teaming is when we look at what an adversary might do in response to certain courses of action. It allows us to evaluate what we could do to prevent, address or respond to their actions. If you don't have plans and contingencies in place it will almost certainly mean the adversary will be at least two steps ahead of you and you will find yourself playing catch up the whole time.'

In a business context, war gaming can enable you to consider stakeholder responses to your crisis management plan. Typically run over two to four hours, a war gaming exercise requires your CMT (sometimes known as the 'blue team') to develop a plan to address the scenario with which they are confronted.

This plan is then presented to the 'red team', a group of role players who represent your stakeholders (for example the media, investors, regulators or competitors).

The red team will then analyse the blue team's plan of action and respond to it in a way that exploits any flaws to make the situation even worse.

Typically played over two or three rounds, the benefits of a war gaming exercise include the ability to develop a robust, well-conceived plan; recognition of the value of considering and planning for future developments; greater creativity and flexibility in responding to a dynamic situation; and a better understanding of how stakeholders may react to your actions. It is also a powerful way to rehearse decision-making.

War gaming is best suited to an experienced CMT that has already participated in the other exercise types. It can be particularly effective in rehearsing your response to a crisis type based on direct conflict, for example an NGO campaign against your business, or malicious product contamination.

Summary

Exercising builds the essential 'muscle memory' to underpin your response to a crisis. It grooves your team and gives them comfort and confidence in the plans and processes they are deploying.

Before commissioning an exercise, take time to understand exactly what you are seeking to achieve with your exercises and select the format accordingly. Doing so will ensure that your exercising programme is purposeful and that your teams get maximum benefit from it.

Run exercises regularly to truly embed capability within your team and to ensure that new team members are fully inducted. It is only through repetition that you will achieve the necessary levels of confidence to see you through a challenging crisis.

Questions

- What are your objectives for exercising? What do you want the outcomes to be?

- What exercise types are best suited to achieving your objectives?

- What is your exercising programme for the next twelve months?

THIRTEEN

How To Ensure Successful Exercise Delivery

'An exercise is supposed to be tough and test your team in a low risk environment. For it to enhance your crisis preparedness it must stretch your team and challenge them to think about things they have not thought about before. If it fails to do that, it's not really adding value.'
— Steven Stewart, Stagecoach Group

I was once running an exercise for leaders of a global financial services business. There were some elements of the scenario with which we were uncomfortable: they seemed a little farfetched, but our client insisted they be retained.

As we introduced one of the more fanciful scenario developments, the team leader pushed back his chair, stood up and said: 'This is ridiculous; that would never happen. I'm not wasting my time on this,' and began to head for the door. In a moment of personal crisis management, I managed to persuade him to continue the exercise while my colleagues in the control room made hasty adjustments to the scenario to avoid further problems.

Running an exercise is itself a risk. As the person responsible for crisis management, your personal credibility is on the line when you invite your senior colleagues to participate in a simulation.

Will they engage with it? Will they find it sufficiently challenging? Will anyone feel exposed or embarrassed by their performance?

If it goes badly, have you lost their support for crisis management training forever?

These are all legitimate concerns but do not let them deter you from running an exercise. The value of exercising is enormous and, by planning well, you can ensure your simulation is developed and delivered flawlessly. Not only that, but a well-run exercise is one of the best ways of securing the long-term support of your senior colleagues for crisis management.

This chapter will explain how to plan and deliver a successful exercise, without jeopardising your career.

Planning

A successful simulation must be realistic and robust. This requires thorough planning. Allow at least six weeks to prepare for a full simulation exercise; develop a comprehensive project management plan to guide you through the process.

Listed below are some of the key considerations and requirements to inform your planning.

Make the experience as near to real life as possible

A simulation can never replicate real life but aim to make it as close as possible. Set up the exercise so it reflects the way in which your organisation operates.

The more realistic the exercise experience, the more immersed your team will become and the more value they will get from it. For example, consider including a realistic online social media platform as part of your exercise. Social media is a key part of any major crisis these days so your team must feel the pressure of being on the receiving end of a social media backlash and have the ability to interact with it in a realistic way.

A simulation is not real life: there will be some artificialities but your aim should be to reduce these to a necessary minimum.

Scenario development

Developing exercises for maximum business value begins with getting the scenario right, a point which Lundin Mining's Jim French endorses:

> 'The practice scenarios we develop differ based on the operation. We factor in whether it's open pit or an underground mine, the size or type of processing plant, the materials used, transportation modes utilised, the operating environment, the dynamics of the local communities, and stakeholder concerns. You can't just develop a generic scenario and say "this applies to all my businesses".'

Choose one of your organisation's critical risks. Most organisations will run no more than a couple of exercises a year. Focus your attention on the most likely and highest impact risks.

The communication director from a global business that caused a major environmental incident explained to me how it had changed his business's approach to simulations.

> 'Now, we always base exercises on our most catastrophic scenarios, our absolute worst nightmares. If you prepare for the worst case, then your ability to deal with any real situation is significantly enhanced. On the other hand, if

you exercise against medium to low level risks and the actual crisis with which you are faced is monumental, it's much harder to scale up your response.'

Your scenario must be extremely challenging, but avoid straying into the territory of a Hollywood script. Senior executives will disengage if the scenario is so outlandish that they simply don't believe it could happen. It needs to be realistic and dramatic, but not fanciful.

Make sure everybody has a role to play and that the exercise requires the expertise of everyone within the room. If the HR director is present and the scenario lacks people implications, it's understandable if they become disengaged.

Your scenario should be multidimensional, not just an operational incident. For example, while a simulation focused on a factory fire presents a business continuity challenge, without other subplots (a faulty sprinkler system, a botched evacuation or falsified fire safety certificates for example) it is too one-dimensional to engage and test your entire team.

A broader context to a scenario is another way to make it more challenging. Imagine the scenario is a cyber-attack. As part of your briefing, you could tell the team that your chief executive is speaking about IT security at a high-profile international conference tomorrow.

Contextual nuggets like this make their challenge that much harder.

Be brave in including organisational failings in your scenario. Without organisational flaws, your team won't face the full challenge and scrutiny they would experience in a real situation. Accept that even successful, well-managed organisations are imperfect and can have things go wrong.

Once the outline of your scenario is clear, write it up as a two-page precis, giving an overview of the plot and its evolution stage by stage with critical twists and turns.

A well-conceived scenario is the essential first step in delivering a successful simulation. Devote quality time and thought to getting it right.

Exercise materials

In addition to the scenario, you must also develop a number of other essential exercise materials. These are:

- The master events list (MEL)
- Exercise inputs
- The exercise brief

Each has an important role to play in the successful delivery of your exercise.

Your scenario forms the basis for your master events list (MEL), a detailed schedule of the sequential developments and associated inputs that will be introduced during the exercise. It is the playbook that summarises how the simulation will unfold on the day.

Inputs (or injects) are the individual events, developments or actions that occur during the simulation. They could be a status report from the scene of an incident, phone calls from colleagues, emails from customers, media enquiries or social media posts.

Inputs should be carefully designed to ensure that all critical crisis management processes and principles are rehearsed. Each input must serve a specific purpose; there's no room for padding. Some are critical updates to move the exercise along. Others are designed to test the decision-making skills of your team. For example, in a cyber exercise the IT director may call your team and tell them:

> 'If we shut down the server, we can guarantee there will be no further contamination of our system. But, if we do that, we can no longer transact via our website and as an ecommerce business that will cost us millions of pounds. What would you like me to do?'

Some inputs may require associated materials – emails, previously prepared media coverage or scripts for role players – to be developed. All should be listed in the MEL.

You should also prepare an exercise brief for role players and the CMT. Both groups of people must be clear about what is expected of them. The exercise brief should include:

- Date, time and location of exercise

- Names and titles of CMT members

- Plan of the exercise location detailing where respective teams are based (whether physically or virtually)

- Names and titles of the role-playing team

- Security protocols and rules of the exercise

- Operating rules for the exercise

- Phone numbers to be used during the exercise

- Email addresses to be used during the exercise

- How to use the online social media platform (if applicable)

- Exercise storyline

- Overview of roles to be played by members of the backroom team

Exercise materials provide the framework for a successful exercise. Invest time and care to ensure they are well conceived, complete and robust.

Logistics

Logistical problems can be distracting and cause frustration during an exercise, so they should play a key part in your planning.

Carefully consider the configuration of your virtual or physical meeting room, telecoms and IT so they support the experience rather than detract from it. Work closely with your facilities management and IT colleagues ahead of the simulation to scope out and deliver the required logistics.

Pay particular attention to how you will handle phone calls and emails. When it comes to calls, you can create exercise-specific phone numbers for maximum control. Alternatively, for greater realism, you can simply have people use their own mobile phones. If you choose the latter option, be aware of the risk of creating an unintended crisis if a team member inadvertently calls someone outside the exercise.

Likewise, it is inadvisable to use participants' normal email addresses for fear of a simulation email being forwarded to a colleague who acts on it in the belief it is a real situation. Instead, consider creating secure email addresses specifically for use in the exercise.

Configuring the virtual or physical exercise rooms and setting up the technology should be carefully considered. Have contingencies and backup plans in case your ideal world situation doesn't work on the day: you don't want the exercise to fail for technological reasons.

Scenario plan what the team may do

To maintain the pace and realism of an exercise, role players must respond quickly to the actions of the CMT. Make their task easier by brainstorming ahead of time the crisis team's likely decisions, information requests and who they may contact.

By scenario planning what the CMT may do, your role players can be flexible and responsive to whatever twists and turns the CMT creates.

Delivery

As the person who has commissioned an exercise, your reputation and credibility depend on how effectively it is delivered.

Achieving a successful outcome for your exercise relies upon creating the right environment and having a skilled team of facilitators and role players to deliver it. Here are some of the key considerations to ensure you achieve these objectives.

Creating the right environment

While a simulation will inevitably create pressure, it should be approached as a learning experience rather than a test. Emphasise to participants that this is a safe and confidential situation. Encourage them to engage fully with the exercise and learn from mistakes.

It is also about identifying where you have gaps in your plan, where further training is needed or additional resources are required. In an exercise, an imperfect response should be viewed positively: it means you have identified areas that need to be addressed in a safe environment with nothing at stake.

As Mark Wenham said: 'The key is that people feel they are in a learning environment rather than a testing one. It allows them to try things out in a safe place where they can learn from their mistakes.'

A spirit of 'psychological safety' is required to enable this. Embrace flaws, learn from them, take action and become more resilient as a result.

Deploy an experienced and confident facilitation team

Your facilitation team – usually an exercise director and an observer – is responsible for choreographing your exercise. They will work in partnership with the backroom team, which is described later.

Based with your CMT, typically they will:

- Introduce the exercise and explain how the simulation will work

- Set out the 'rules of the game' and security protocols

- Observe the performance of the team as they manage the scenario

- Liaise and coordinate with the backroom controller

- Call timeouts if necessary, to re-orientate the team

- Run the exercise debrief

As a consequence, they must command the respect of the CMT, know when to intervene and when to step back, identify key issues in the team's response and lead the debrief session with courage, authority and credibility.

Even in a simulation, the pressure is real and so having a clear, calm, credible, empathetic exercise director is essential. They need to have the nous, sensitivity and confidence to read the room, sense whether the team is flying or struggling and turn the pressure up or down accordingly.

Assigning a consultancy partner to this role can be a good idea as it is often easier for them to give your leadership team challenging feedback.

Assemble a knowledgeable, well-organised and unflappable backroom team

The backroom team (or inject cell) is invisible to the CMT but the success of your exercise is dependent upon their qualities and capabilities.

This group of people will comprise six or more role players who are corralled by a backroom controller. Some should be members of your team who are subject matter experts and role play, for instance, colleagues, regulators or customers. Others are from outside your organisation and represent key stakeholders, for example, a journalist or an ex-police officer role-playing emergency services.

Role players must have not just the right technical expertise but also the right temperament. They will be placed under severe pressure during the exercise and need to stay cool as the CMT begins to make demands of them.

It can feel a little uncomfortable for role players who find themselves on the receiving end of this pressure so you need a team of people who are not only knowledgeable, but also well organised, calm and nimble.

It is the responsibility of the backroom controller to manage this pressurised environment and keep their role players on track. That means ensuring that scheduled inputs reach the CMT in the right order and at the right time, and that incoming calls from the CMT are logged and responded to. Sometimes they will need to make unplanned changes to the running order of the simulation 'on the fly'. It requires an unflappable, well-organised individual with strong communication skills to successfully fulfil this role.

The backroom controller and their team of role players are the engine room for your exercise. Securing the right people to take on this responsibility is one of the keys to a successful exercise.

Be flexible and responsive to the actions of the team

You cannot predict every decision, action and response of your CMT. Your facilitation and backroom team must be sufficiently smart and agile to flex when the simulation takes an unexpected turn. The evolution of a simulation cannot be set in tablets of stone.

It's up to the facilitator to be responsive and flexible to whatever the CMT chooses to do. It's unacceptable for them to say in the middle of a simulation: 'Timeout. You can't do that. That isn't in the scenario.' Doing so risks the team completely disengaging with the exercise.

They should also be prepared to turn up the pressure if your team is finding the challenge too easy.

One way of doing this during the exercise is simply to increase the volume of questions and inputs from stakeholders. Can the team deal with the tsunami of enquiries? Can they prioritise them? Can they make sense of the information and identify what matters most?

Another curve ball can be to engineer the removal of your CEO from the CMT by, for example, requiring them to fly to head office to update your group board. Another team member is then required to step up and assume the leadership role. Taking this approach tests the effectiveness of your handover procedures and rehearses how your team operates in the absence of its expected leader.

Stagecoach's Steven Stewart is a fan of this approach for the following reason: 'When a crisis strikes, you can bet your CEO will be on holiday or on a plane. So always include deputies in your crisis exercises as, quite often, they turn out to be the people in the front line.'

It's not up to the CMT to follow your script; it is the responsibility of the facilitation team to be responsive to it.

Summary

Exercises are among the most important elements of your crisis management programme. However, they are challenging to develop and deliver.

Thorough planning is essential to ensure that your exercise delivers against its objectives. Couple this with a supportive learning environment, skilled facilitation and well-marshalled role players and you will significantly increase your team's confidence and capabilities.

Questions

- How frequently will you run exercises? How much time will you dedicate to them?

- List three potential exercise scenarios for your organisation.

- In each case, what developments could you introduce to increase pressure on the team?

- Which stakeholders would need to be represented by role players?

- Who could you use to facilitate the exercise (and provide honest feedback to your leadership team)?

SECTION SIX
RESPONSE

FOURTEEN

Fundamentals Of A Successful Crisis Response

'There can't be a crisis next week, my schedule is already full.'
— Henry Kissinger

A crisis poses the acid test of management. Doing and saying the right thing confidently and quickly when crisis strikes is critical to minimise the impact on your business.

This book focuses primarily on the development and rehearsal of crisis management plans to prevent and prepare for crisis situations. But, ultimately, reputations are preserved or destroyed as a result of what people do and say under intense pressure when crisis strikes. On the worst day of their lives, leaders must rise to this challenge, or risk losing everything.

More than twenty-five years' experience working with CMTs around the world means I know where teams most often falter and which mistakes will have most impact on the quality of their response.

Here are my ten tips for responding surefootedly to even the most challenging of situations.

1. Activate your team without delay

When the early signs of a potential crisis are identified, there's a temptation to hope it fizzles out before any damage is done. The danger of this is that, if instead of fizzling out the situation explodes, you end up chasing the situation rather than driving it.

Make sure everyone in the organisation knows who to tell if they spot a problem so that word reaches the right people as quickly as possible. Establish a process for notifying executives of CMT activation and set up a dedicated CMT teleconference facility and online meeting place.

Be prepared to activate and prepare your crisis team at the first whiff of a serious incident. Much better to stand the team down if it turns out to be a false alarm than to forever play catch up.

2. Follow your plan

Many's the time I've seen a carefully prepared crisis management plan left unopened on a CMT table. Equally, I've observed plenty of CMTs applying an ad hoc approach to crisis management when under intense pressure.

Your crisis plan has been written for a reason and the ways of working you rehearsed through exercises have been proven to work. Don't go 'off piste'. Stay true to the framework outlined in your crisis management plan to work purposefully and make best progress.

3. Team and meeting discipline

Time is short in a crisis so you need to use it wisely. Stick to your meeting agenda. Make sure everyone's voice is heard, but not all at the same time. Be respectful of each other's points of view. Be brief and to the point. Stick to the time allowed for the meeting.

4. Set your strategic intent

Your leadership team should never begin developing an action plan before agreeing its strategic intent. Strategic intent is a single-minded articulation of what success looks like, the end goal for your crisis management efforts. It could be as simple as 'to retain the trust of our customers'. Having a clear strategic intent understood by everyone involved in your crisis response enables you to prioritise your efforts and guide your decision-making.

It's a concept that is endorsed by Guy Esnouf: 'What are the objectives? I've sat in crisis rooms in different countries and different companies where there has been this paralysis because it wasn't clear exactly what we wanted to do.'

As mentioned in Chapter 7, consider drafting 'in principle' strategic intents against your critical risks as part of your scenario planning process for verification when a crisis breaks.

5. Determine your 'main effort' (priority areas for focus)

In a crisis you will never have as much resource as you would ideally like, so you must choose where and how you apply it. The CMT should explicitly determine and communicate the 'main effort' (in other words the priority area of focus) to guide their actions and those of teams working at an operational level.

This ensures that teams at all levels are focused on the same priority at the same time. Your main effort should be reviewed and revised during the evolution of the crisis.

6. Ensure clarity of roles and responsibilities

Problems occur when roles and responsibilities for crisis response are unclear, either within a CMT or across different parts of your business. At a time when resource is in short supply and you need to work with great purpose, you cannot afford duplication of effort or, even worse, conflicting actions between different parts of the business.

Be explicit about who is doing what on the team and the respective responsibilities of different parts of the business. Have people play back to you what they have heard to ensure the message has been successfully conveyed. There is no room for ambiguity in a crisis.

7. Conduct regular check-ins and re-evaluation

Crises develop at breakneck speed so you must ensure your entire team remains on 'the same page'. This requires regular, rapid check-ins to re-evaluate status, review actions and agree what needs to be done next.

Without this discipline you may find yourself managing the crisis as it was eight hours ago, rather than the reality now.

Beware the 'creeping crisis', which gets incrementally worse without anyone really noticing that it has developed into a much bigger, more serious crisis than it originally appeared.

8. Engage in scenario planning

Crisis management best practice suggests that you should 'set the narrative' or 'shape the agenda'. Certainly, you should avoid being reactive, simply following or responding to events as they unfold. The best way to do this is through scenario planning.

Assign a couple of colleagues (your most 'creative pessimists') to spend time in a darkened room considering where the situation could go to next and the worst-case outcomes. By bringing their conclusions back to the CMT they can help it make decisions that will shape events in a more positive direction.

Scenario planning also enables the team to prepare contingencies in the event of the worst-case scenario coming true.

9. Be courageous in making timely decisions

Crisis management is a high-stakes activity in which every decision can have significant and long-lasting implications for your business. It's not surprising that some business leaders delay decision-making until all the facts are clear. Sadly, this is usually too late to protect a business's reputation.

In a crisis there is rarely a perfect decision; sometimes it's simply about making the least bad decision. The leader's responsibility is to make the best decision they can with the information they have at that time, and to do so without unnecessary delay.

As Mark Wenham puts it: 'People will often shy away from making a decision, hoping the problem will go away. Before they know it, the situation is even worse. In a crisis, even when everything is against you, when you lack the information you want, you must have the courage to make a decision.'

Always remember: the worst decision in a crisis is no decision at all.

10. Be true to your values

In a public, highly pressurised environment, a crisis reveals whether values so proudly trumpeted on an organisation's website are authentic or simply corporate puff. Oxford Metrica's research found that organisations which acted contrary to their values during a crisis suffered the most damage. Consequently, your values must underpin your crisis response.

As Jeni Britton Bauer, owner of Jeni's Splendid Ice Creams, which had to recall 265 tons of contaminated ice cream in April 2015, told Sarah Lawson: 'Values exist in the great times, but they also exist in the shitty times. If you abandon those during the worst times, then they're not yours really.'

Mark Wenham concurs: 'Doing the right thing is usually different from the easy option or obvious solution. It's being selfless: understanding that it's not about you, it's about your organisation and its stakeholders.'

Summary

Planning, training and exercising give organisations the capabilities and confidence to succeed in a crisis. However, the unique pressure of a real crisis and its extraordinarily high stakes results in predictable mistakes being made time and time again.

Be aware of the pitfalls, stay true to what you have learned through your planning and training programme, adhere to the ten golden rules in this chapter and you will prevail.

Questions

- Which of these ten golden rules resonates most strongly with you? Why?

- Which golden rule is your organisation most likely to transgress? Why? How could you avoid this happening?

- What golden rule would you add to the list?

FIFTEEN

How To Continuously Improve

'Never let a good crisis go to waste.'
    — Unknown

Complacency is the enemy of crisis management. The moment you think you've got it cracked is the moment you are most likely to be sideswiped.

A truly crisis resistant culture requires a commitment to constant learning and improvement. Actively seek out flaws and gaps in your current crisis management capability; anything that can be identified and addressed ahead of a live incident makes you more crisis proof.

Treat exercises as an opportunity not just to rehearse but also to enhance your resilience. Take time to thoroughly review and make changes based on what you learn from real incidents.

As Sue Boxall observes, taking such an approach can have deep and long-lasting benefits:

> 'Addressing lessons learned from training is a really effective way of keeping the subject of crisis management alive between training and exercising sessions. Working through action plans and follow ups demonstrate that the business is really committed and interested in getting crisis management right. It shows it's not just a box ticking exercise or means of keeping the board happy.'

Investing time in crisis management planning, training and exercising gives you a platform for success; committing to continuous learning and improvement will make you truly crisis resistant.

This chapter explains some of the key ways in which you can ensure this happens.

Crisis management policy

Continuous improvement begins by creating a crisis management policy, signed by your CEO, which sets out the requirements for crisis management at your business.

It will include, for example, the requirement to maintain and update your crisis management plan, a commitment to training team members and a requirement to complete a minimum number of exercises per year.

As Lidl's Aoife Clarke explains:

> 'We don't treat crisis management as a project with a start and end date because it's something that should always be front of mind. Likewise, we never view our crisis management plan as a static document. We are constantly looking at it: I set regular calendar reminders to check the contacts are complete, accurate and up to date and to consider whether there are new scenarios which should be included.'

Crucially, your crisis management policy should also state that the results of any incidents, simulations, activation call-outs, emergency response training drills and desktop exercises must be documented to include lessons learned and actions taken to improve crisis management effectiveness.

Learning from exercises

Remember (and reinforce to your colleagues) that exercises should be viewed as rehearsals, a means to improve, not as tests. No one should be expected to perform flawlessly in an exercise; indeed, the real value of an exercise is in the learnings derived from it.

Treat exercises as safe opportunities to make mistakes and identify flaws to be addressed so you can enhance your crisis resilience.

A simulation is draining, and sometimes emotional. Nevertheless, you *must* make time immediately after the exercise to gather feedback. Don't spend three hours immersed in the exercise and fifteen minutes taking feedback: at least forty-five minutes are required to secure immediate feedback (the 'hot debrief'). Capturing the CMT's thoughts and feelings while still fresh in their minds is of paramount importance. It is also an effective way of 'coming down' from the exercise and returning to the 'real world'.

When running the exercise debrief, the facilitator should ask participants to consider and share:

- Their overall impressions of how the team performed

- What they felt they did particularly well

- Areas for attention or improvement

- Specific actions or next steps to be taken subsequent to the exercise

Ensure that all feedback is faithfully captured and invite participants to reflect on their experience and send any subsequent thoughts to the exercise facilitator.

A post-exercise report (PXR) should be produced based on the facilitation team's assessment of how the team responded to the scenario, along with the views and actions identified by the team themselves.

A typical post-exercise report should include:

- An executive summary outlining overall findings
- An overview of the exercise including the scenario and participants
- Feedback and recommendations against key criteria including:
    - Crisis recognition
    - Setting of strategic direction
    - Action planning/prioritisation
    - Team organisation, culture and leadership
    - Information gathering and situational awareness
    - Decision-making
    - Communication
- Actions/next steps with deadlines and accountability assigned

An effective simulation will generate many actions, including changes to the plan, training requirements and additional resource requirements. These should be speedily implemented to capitalise on the momentum generated by the exercise.

As the person accountable for crisis management, it is your responsibility to ensure all agreed actions are implemented. If not, flaws that emerged in the exercise will derail you during a real crisis when the stakes are so much higher.

Remember also to review the simulation itself in terms of how successfully it met your original objectives. Run a debrief with the facilitation team, take feedback from participants and identify ways in which future exercise delivery can be improved.

Learning from live incidents

Much time and effort go into developing and embedding a crisis management plan, but no matter how diligently you work to perfect your plan, there is only one true test of its efficacy: a live crisis.

When a crisis breaks, your team is called to action, your plan is deployed, your crisis leader must make the big decisions and your spokesperson must address the media. This is the moment when you will discover whether your plan works or not and the true capabilities of your CMT members will become clear.

A live crisis is, therefore, an invaluable learning experience, which you must not waste. Tempting though it may be, never return to business as usual in the aftermath of a crisis without taking time to identify and act on the learnings it revealed. Instead, view the crisis as a unique opportunity to further build your crisis resilience.

As NFU Mutual's Jo Lumani advises:

> 'It's difficult to be objective and dispassionate in the midst of a crisis which is why, after the event, reflection is so important. You never deliver a perfect crisis response, so you should evaluate, learn and build on those situations to improve your performance next time. It's hard to remember all of the learnings once the crisis is over. So, during the crisis keep a contemporaneous record of what didn't go according to plan, resources you wished you'd had, gaps and flaws in your plan. Take feedback from colleagues, the media and other stakeholders to help inform the way you do things in future.'

Schedule a post-crisis review meeting to be attended by the main people involved in your crisis response. Pre-brief them to consider and bring with them to the meeting their key learnings from the incident.

Crucially, the meeting must take place in a spirit of psychological safety. The objective must always be to identify and act on learnings, not to point the finger of blame. A strong, fair and independent chairperson is essential to maintain this focus.

Use the following agenda template to guide your post-crisis review meeting.

Crisis management plan

- What worked well?

- What could be improved?

- What was missing?

Crisis management team

- How quickly and effectively did you identify the initial incident? How could this be improved?

- How quickly and effectively was the team activated? How could this be improved?

- Did you have the right people/expertise in the room? Who/what else would have been useful?

- How effectively did you work together? How could this be improved?

- How did your decision-making processes work?

- With hindsight, did you make the best decisions? If not, why not?

- How effectively were information, actions and decisions logged? Was everyone clear about the latest situation and decisions/actions taken?

People

- How did your extended team perform?

- Did you have sufficient human resource?

- What could be improved?

- Have you identified any training needs?

- How did any suppliers/partners/other key stakeholders perform?

- Do you need any additional/alternative suppliers?

Communication

- How well did you handle stakeholder (employees, media, customers, investors, regulators, etc) communication?

- How did your spokespeople perform? Is further media training required?

- What changes do you need to make in the handling of communication?

Resources

- How did your technical, physical and logistical resources work in practice?

- Does anything require upgrading/enhancing?

- Was anything missing?

- Do you need to invest in any additional resources?

Other

- What else could we do to perform better in the event of future crises?

Never leave the meeting without agreeing next steps with deadlines and accountability for actioning them. As the person responsible for crisis management it is also your responsibility to follow up and ensure that actions have been completed.

Create opportunities to learn not just from real incidents but also near misses and the experience of others within your industry. As Cathay Pacific's Gus Whitcomb says:

> 'The airline industry is very competitive but the one area where there isn't antitrust regulation is in sharing learnings about accident response. We actively work with other airlines to compare plans and share ideas. But I also talk to train, railroad and bus operators because, while they also operate in the transportation sector, they deal with different things that I haven't even thought about. I'll even talk with companies that have nothing to do with our sector because an active shooter or terrorist attack can happen to any organisation, not just an airline or an airport. I'll to go to any

place where I can meet people to share and learn from each other.'

Summary

Getting through a crisis successfully sucks every last drop of energy from those involved: it occupies every waking minute (and sometimes their dreams too). When the heat of the crisis subsides, it's tempting to move on as quickly as possible. Resist this temptation or else you may leave unresolved vulnerabilities in the system.

Make sure everyone is briefed on lessons learned to ensure that future incidents are prevented or handled more effectively. As Sue Boxall says: 'If you work for a multi-site organisation, sharing lessons learned and improvements across the whole business is really helpful.'

Take the same approach to exercising: its value is as much in the steps you take after a simulation as in the time spent during the exercise itself. Be creative in creating opportunities to learn and share experience. Sue Boxall again: 'Consider inviting members of one site's CMT to another location's training workshops to cross-fertilise knowledge, learnings and experience.'

Never believe that your crisis management plan is complete. A process of continual improvement and a growth mindset are the hallmarks of truly resilient organisations.

Questions

- What are the key requirements of your crisis management policy? Did you meet them over the last twelve months?

- What were the key learnings from your most recent exercise? Have all actions been completed? If not, attend to them now.

- What were the key learnings from your most recent crisis, incident or near miss? Have they been acted upon?

- What is the biggest crisis to hit one of your competitors over the last five years? What can you learn from their response?

- What three actions would make the biggest difference to enhancing your crisis preparedness?

SIXTEEN

Concluding Thoughts

'While the world is an unpredictable place,
unpredictability is often not the problem. The
problem is that faced with clear risks, we still fail to
act.'
— Tim Harford

This book was written in 2020 as the world, its people, governments and businesses faced the biggest crisis in living memory, COVID-19. The virus's devastating impact illustrates the power of a crisis to wreak extraordinary harm on people and organisations.

There are few silver linings coming out of the pandemic but, if it serves as a wake-up call for more organisations to plan, train and rehearse for crisis, that will be a positive and important by-product.

My twenty-five years of experience tell me that organisations that identify the risks they face and take action to prepare for them are quicker, more purposeful and ultimately more effective in their crisis response. Consequently, they preserve lives, livelihoods, value and reputation.

Follow the principles and structures outlined in this book and you will not only successfully fulfil your crisis management responsibilities, you will also create organisational capability and confidence of immeasurable value.

It is this capability and confidence that enables your leaders to do and say the right things on the worst day of their careers and prevent the needless harm that would otherwise result.

Being accountable for crisis management does indeed bring great responsibility. But it should also be a source of pride that your efforts will make a huge difference, not just to your organisation, but also to the lives and livelihoods of all those affected by it.

References

Chapter 1

BBC (2015) 'Alton Towers Smiler crash: four seriously hurt', *BBC News*. Available at: www.bbc.co.uk/news /uk-32980354 (Accessed: 2 October 2020)

BBC (2015) 'Corfu children's deaths: Thomas Cook breached "duty of care"', *BBC News*. Available at: www .bbc.co.uk/news/uk-england-32719823 (Accessed: 2 October 2020)

BBC (2020) 'Travelex boss breaks silence 17 days after cyber-attack', *BBC News*. Available at: www.bbc.co.uk /news/business-51152151 (Accessed: 2 October 2020)

Bushey, C, and Meyer, G (2020) 'Boeing expects 737 MAX crisis costs to reach $18.6bn', *Financial Times*. Available at: www.ft.com/content/0e9a99de-428d -11ea-a43a-c4b328d9061c (Accessed: 2 October 2020)

Davies, N (2015) 'Marikana massacre: The untold story of the strike leader who died for workers' rights', *The Guardian*. Available at: www.theguardian.com/world /2015/may/19/marikana-massacre-untold-story-strike -leader-died-workers-rights (Accessed: 19 May 2020)

Ewing, J (2016) 'Volkswagen memos suggest company misled US regulators', *New York Times*. Available at: www.nytimes.com/2016/02/19/business/volkswagen -memos-suggest-emissions-problem-was-known-earlier .html?auth=login-google&login=google&module= inline (Accessed: 19 May 2020)

Freshfields Bruckhaus Deringer (2013) 'Containing a crisis. Dealing with corporate disasters in the digital age', Freshfields Bruckhaus Deringer LLP. Available at: www.freshfields.com/49fabb/globalassets/campaign -landing/cyber-security/containing-a-crisis.pdf (Accessed: 2 October 2020)

Jones, R (2020) 'Travelex forced to take down website after cyber-attack', *The Guardian*. Available at: www .theguardian.com/technology/2020/jan/02/travelex -forced-to-take-down-website-after-cyber-attack (Accessed: 2 October 2020)

Knight, R and Pretty, D (2001) 'Reputation and Value: The case of corporate catastrophes', Oxford Metrica. Available at: http://www.oxfordmetrica.com/public /CMS/Files/488/01RepComAIG.pdf

Press Association (2015) 'Thomas Cook CEO refuses to say sorry for deaths as ex-boss declines questions', *The Guardian*. Available at: www.theguardian.com/uk-news/2015/may/07/ex-thomas-cook-boss-refuses-to-answer-questions-over-childrens-deaths (Accessed: 2 October 2020)

Stevens, M (2019) 'Whirlpool recall of fire risk tumble dryers begins today', *Which?* Available at: www.which.co.uk/news/2019/07/whirlpool-recall-of-fire-risk-tumble-dryers-begins-today (Accessed: 27 May 2020)

Stewart, S, interview (28 April 2020)

Thomas, L (2017) 'United CEO says airline had to "re-accommodate" passenger, and the reaction was wild', CNBC. Available at: www.cnbc.com/2017/04/10/united-ceo-says-airline-had-to-re-accommodate-passenger-and-twitter-is-having-a-riot.html (Accessed: 2 October 2020)

Travelex UK (2020) 'Statement on IT issues affecting Travelex Services' [Tweet]. Available at: https://twitter.com/TravelexUK/status/1212840156480315401 (Accessed: 2 October 2020)

TSB (2019) 'TSB announces 2018 full year results', TSB Bank. Available at: www.tsb.co.uk/news-releases/tsb-announces-2018-full-year-results (Accessed: 2 October 2020)

Vincent, M (2016) 'Samsung's fiddling while phone burns is better than most', *Financial Times.* Available at: www.ft.com/content/05c8c566-9209-11e6-a72e -b428cb934b78 (Accessed: 19 May 2020)

Whitcomb, G, interview (13 May 2019)

Chapter 2

Boxall, S, interview (8 October 2020)

BSI (2018) 'Crisis management. Guidance for developing a strategic capability', British Standards Institution. Available at: https://shop.bsigroup.com/ProductDetail/ ?pid=000000000030339232

Covey, S, interview (15 May 2020)

French, J, interview (4 May 2020)

ISO (2009) 'ISO GUIDE 73:2009. Risk Management – Vocabulary', International Organization for Standardization. Available at: www.iso.org/obp/ui/#iso:std:iso: guide:73:ed-1:v1:en (Accessed: 2 October 2020)

ISO (2019) 'ISO 22301:2019. Security and Resilience – Business Continuity Management Systems – Requirements', International Organization for Standardization. Available at: www.iso.org/obp/ui#iso:std:iso:22301:ed -2:v1:en (Accessed: 2 October 2020)

Ready (2020) 'Emergency response plan', Ready. Available at: www.ready.gov/business/implementation/emergency (Accessed: 2 October 2020)

Stewart, S, interview (28 April 2020)

Whitcomb, G, interview (13 May 2019)

Chapter 3

BSI (2018) 'Crisis management. Guidance for developing a strategic capability', British Standards Institution.

Covey, S, interview (15 May 2020)

Lumani, J, interview (27 April 2020)

Pitts, G (2008) 'The testing of Michael McCain', *The Globe and Mail*. Available at: www.theglobeandmail.com/report-on-business/the-testing-of-michael-mccain/article598005 (Accessed: 19 October 2020)

Ratner, G, interview (28 August 2019)

Stewart, S, interview (28 April 2020)

Suesser, K, interview (11 May 2020)

Chapter 4

BBC (2014) 'Virgin Galactic spacecraft crash kills pilot', *BBC News*. Available at: www.bbc.co.uk/news/world -us-canada-29857182 (Accessed: 2 October 2020)

BBC (2019) 'Horsemeat scandal: Trial of firms accused of selling horse as beef opens in Paris', *BBC News*. Available at: www.bbc.co.uk/news/world-europe -46951855

Beasley, S (2019) 'Boeing CEO ousting inevitable, amid poor marks from regulators and crash victims', *Politico*. Available at: www.politico.com/news/2019 /12/23/boeing-ceo-dennis-muilenburg-resigns-089555 (Accessed: 5 October 2020)

Boxall, S, interview (8 October 2020)

Clarke, A, interview (30 April 2020)

Crockett, Z (2018) 'How to lose $1B in 10 seconds', The Hustle. Available at: https://thehustle.co/gerald-ratners -billion-dollar-speech (Accessed: 5 October 2020)

Equifax (2016) 'Stock chart and quote', Equifax. Available at: https://investor.equifax.com/stock-information /stock-chart-and-quote (Accessed: 5 October 2020)

French, J, interview (4 May 2020)

Institute of Directors (2013) Gerald Ratner speaking at the 1991 Institute of Directors Annual Convention. Available at: www.youtube.com/watch?v=Nj9BZz71yQE (Accessed: 5 October 2020)

Milmo, D (2007) 'One dead, many hurt as train derails at 95mph', *The Guardian*. Available at: www.theguardian.com/uk/2007/feb/24/transport.world (Accessed: 2 October 2020)

Ratner, G, interview (28 August 2019)

Reuters (2018) 'CEO of UK's TSB bank drafts in IBM to fix online banking problems', Reuters. Available at: https://fr.reuters.com/article/britain-tsb-idINKBN1HX0SD (Accessed: 17 September 2020)

Sommerlad, J (2019) 'Kegworth air disaster: What happened and how did the plane crash change airline safety?', *The Independent*. Available at: www.independent.co.uk/news/uk/home-news/kegworth-air-disaster-30th-anniversary-boeing-midland-737-leicestershire-plane-crash-a8717656.html (Accessed: 2 October 2020)

Volkswagen (2015) 'Share price information', Volkswagen AG. Available at: www.volkswagenag.com/en/InvestorRelations/shares/interactive-share-price-monitor.html (Accessed: 5 October 2020)

Webb, T (2010) 'BP's clumsy response to oil spill threatens to make a bad situation worse', *The Guardian*. Available at: www.theguardian.com/business/2010/jun /01/bp-response-oil-spill-tony-hayward (Accessed: 5 October 2020)

Whitcomb, G, interview (13 May 2019)

Chapter 5

BBC (2016) 'Bad Aibling train crash: German controller jailed', *BBC News*. Available at: www.bbc.co.uk/news /world-europe-38206468 (Accessed: 17 September 2020)

Booth, R, Weaver, M and McCurry, J (2010) 'Toyota recall: 250 UK cases reported, 20 stuck pedals found, and one accident injury claimed', *The Guardian*. Available at: www.theguardian.com/business/2010/feb/04 /toyota-recall-accelerator-fault (Accessed: 5 October 2020)

Boxall, S, interview (8 October 2020)

Calvert, J, Arbuthnott, G and Leake, J (2020) 'Coronavirus: 38 days when Britain sleepwalked into disaster', *The Sunday Times*. Available at: www.thetimes.co.uk/article /coronavirus-38-days-when-britain-sleepwalked-into -disaster-hq3b9tlgh (Accessed: 17 September 2020)

Clarke, A, interview (30 April 2020)

Collingridge, A (2019) 'Boeing and Airbus battle for the skies', *The Sunday Times*. Available at: www.thetimes .co.uk/article/boeing-and-airbus-battle-for-the-skies -z9c60xkb5 (Accessed: 17 September 2020)

Dean, J (2020) '737 MAX plane was built by "clowns and monkeys", claim Boeing workers', *The Times*. Available at: www.thetimes.co.uk/article/737-max-plane-was -built-by-clowns-and-monkeys-claim-boeing-workers -czk3txqq2 (Accessed: 17 September 2020)

Freed, J and Rucinski, T (2020) 'Factbox: in Boeing internal messages, employees distrust the 737 MAX and mock regulators', Reuters. Available at: https://uk .reuters.com/article/uk-boeing-737max-factbox/factbox -in-boeing-internal-messages-employees-distrust-the -737-max-and-mock-regulators-idUKKBN1Z90NN?fee dType=RSS&feedName=businessNews (Accessed: 17 September 2020)

The House Committee on Transportation and Infra-structure (2020) 'Final committee report: the design, development and certification of the Boeing 737 MAX', The House Committee on Transportation and Infra-structure. Available at: https://transportation.house.gov /imo/media/doc/2020.09.15%20FINAL%20737%20MAX %20Report%20for%20Public%20Release.pdf (Accessed: 5 October 2020)

King, J (2015). 'Thomas Cook Group PLC: review of customer health, safety, welfare, relations and crisis management', Justin King [independent reviewer]. Available at: www.policyconnect.org.uk/appcog/sites /site_appcog/files/news/558/fieldnewsdownloads /thomascooknov2015justin-king-independent-review .pdf (Accessed: 5 October 2020)

Rothfeder, J (2016) 'The Volkswagen settlement: how bad management leads to big punishment', *The New Yorker*. Available at: www.newyorker.com/business /currency/the-volkswagen-settlement-how-bad -management-leads-to-big-punishment (Accessed: 5 October 2020)

Ruiz, R and Mather, V (2015) 'The FIFA scandal: what's happened, and what's to come', *The New York Times*. Available at: www.nytimes.com/2015/09/26/sports /soccer/the-fifa-scandal-whats-happened-and-whats -to-come.html (Accessed: 5 October 2020)

Segal, T (2020) 'Enron scandal: the fall of a Wall Street darling', Investopedia. Available at: www.investopedia .com/updates/enron-scandal-summary (Accessed: 5 October 2020)

Chapter 6

Bain, M (2017) 'Nike is facing a new wave of anti-sweatshop protests', Quartz. Available at: https:// qz.com/1042298/nike-is-facing-a-new-wave-of-anti -sweatshop-protests (Accessed: 5 October 2020)

BBC News (2014) 'Phone-hacking case explained', BBC News. Available at: www.bbc.co.uk/news/uk-24894403 (Accessed: 9 December 2020)

Dawkins, D (2019) 'Virgin billionaire Branson attacked in parliament over staff pay during Coronoavirus - but employees remain supportive', *Forbes*. Available at: www.forbes.com/sites/daviddawkins/2020/03/19 /virgin-billionaire-branson-attacked-in-parliament -over-staff-pay-during-coronavirus-crisisbut-employ- ees-remain-supportive/?sh=e1d00bc3b8f5 (Accessed: 5 October 2020)

Knight, R and Pretty, D 'Reputation and Value: The case of corporate catastrophes', Oxford Metrica

McDougall, D (2008) 'The hidden face of Primark fash- ion', *The Guardian*. Available at: www.theguardian.com /world/2008/jun/22/india.humanrights (Accessed: 5 October 2020)

Chapter 7

BBC: Don't Tell Me the Score (2019) Culture: Sir Clive Woodward [podcast]. Available at: www.bbc.co.uk /programmes/p07xb7lm (Accessed: 5 October 2020)

Lumani, J, interview (27 April 2020)

Ripley, A (2005) 'How to get out alive: what the science of evacuation reveals about how humans behave in the worst of times', *Time*. Available at: http://content.time.com/time/magazine/article/0,9171,1053663-3,00.html (Accessed: 19 October 2020)

Smith, P (2017) 'The true story behind the deadliest air disaster of all time', *The Telegraph*. Available at: www.telegraph.co.uk/travel/comment/tenerife-airport-disaster (Accessed: 19 May 2020)

Suesser, K, interview (11 May 2020)

Whitcomb, G, interview (13 May 2020)

Chapter 8

French, J, interview (4 May 2020)

Gosnell, C, interview (15 May 2020)

Green, K (2015) '3 things pilots know about crisis management', Fast Company. Available at: www.fastcompany.com/3053896/3-things-pilots-know-about-crisis-management (Accessed: 5 October 2020)

McGuinness, E, interview (4 May 2020)

Rivera, K and Stainback, D (2019) 'PwC's Global Crisis Survey 2019: Crisis preparedness as the next competitive advantage: learning from 4,500 crises', PwC. Available at: www.pwc.com/gx/en/forensics /global-crisis-survey/pdf/pwc-global-crisis-survey -2019.pdf (Accessed: 17 September 2020)

Whitcomb, G, interview (13 May 2020)

Chapter 9

Briggs, B (2019) 'Hackers hit Norsk Hydro with ransomware. The company responded with transparency', Microsoft. Available at: https://news.microsoft .com/transform/hackers-hit-norsk-hydro-ransomware -company-responded-transparency (Accessed: 18 September 2020)

Esnouf, G, interview (18 January 2017)

Goodin, D (2019) '"Severe" ransomware attack cripples big aluminium producer', Ars Technica. Available at: https://arstechnica.com/information-technology/2019 /03/severe-ransomware-attack-cripples-big-aluminum -producer (Accessed: 5 October 2020)

Norsk Hydro (2019) *Why Hydro chose to be transparent during cyber-attack* [Video]. Available at: https:// www.youtube.com/watch?v=C6MDz-AgQuE&t=3s (Accessed: 6 October 2020)

Oxford Metrica, 'Reputation Review, 2011', Oxford Metrica. Available at: www.oxfordmetrica.com/public/CMS /Files/825/Aon_Oxford%20Metrica%20Reputation %20Review_2011.pdf

Stewart, S, interview (28 April 2020)

Whitcomb, G, interview (13 May 2019)

Chapter 10

French, J, interview (4 May 2020)

Lumani, J, interview (27 April 2020)

McGuinness, E, interview (4 May 2020)

Stewart, S, interview (28 April 2020)

Suesser, K, interview (11 May 2020)

Chapter 11

Clarke, A, interview (30 April 2020)

Green, K (2015) '3 things pilots know about crisis management', Fast Company. Available at: www .fastcompany.com/3053896/3-things-pilots-know-about -crisis-management (Accessed: 5 October 2020)

Webb, T (2010) 'BP's clumsy response to oil spill threatens to make a bad situation worse', *The Guardian*. Available at: www.theguardian.com/business/2010/jun/01/bp-response-oil-spill-tony-hayward (Accessed: 5 October 2020)

Wenham, M, interview (21 April 2015)

Chapter 12

BBC Worldwide (2017). *Astronauts: Do you have what it takes?* [Television programme]. BBC Two

BBC (2019) 'Train named after Cornish 9/11 hero Rick Rescorla', *BBC News*. Available at: www.bbc.co.uk/news/uk-england-cornwall-47866351 (Accessed: 7 September 2020)

French, J, interview (4 May 2020)

Gladwell, M (2008) *Outliers*. New York: Little, Brown and Company

Lumani, J, interview (27 April 2020)

McGuinness, E, interview (4 May 2020)

Stewart, J (2002) 'The real heroes are dead', *The New Yorker*. Available at: www.newyorker.com/magazine

/2002/02/11/the-real-heroes-are-dead (Accessed: 5 October 2020)

Wenham, M, interview (21 April 2015)

Whitcomb, G, interview (13 May 2020)

Chapter 13

French, J, interview (4 May 2020)

Stewart, S, interview (28 April 2020)

Wenham, M, interview (21 April 2015)

Chapter 14

Esnouf, G, interview (18 January 2017)

Knight, R and Pretty, D 'Reputation and Value: The case of corporate catastrophes', Oxford Metrica

Lawson, S (2015) 'Crisis management advice for the ages: "Own it, even if it sucks"', Fast Company. Available at: www.fastcompany.com/3048050/crisis -management-advice-for-the-ages-own-it-even-if-it -sucks (Accessed: 18 September 2020)

Wenham, M, interview (21 April 2015)

Chapter 15

Boxall, S, interview (8 October 2020)

Clarke, A, interview (30 April 2020)

Lumani, J, interview (27 April 2020)

Whitcomb, G, interview (13 May 2019)

Chapter 16

Harford, T (2020) 'Why we fail to prepare for disasters', *Financial Times*. Available at: www.ft.com/content/74e5f04a-7df1-11ea-82f6-150830b3b99a (Accessed: 19 October 2020)

Acknowledgements

I would like to thank everyone who enabled me to write this book despite the disruption, uncertainties and challenges caused by the COVID-19 outbreak.

I am sincerely grateful to Pavel Albores, Aoife Clarke, Steve Covey, Guy Esnouf, Dennis Flynn, Jim French, Claire Gosnell, Jo Lumani, Eilish McGuinness, Paul Newman, Steve Parkinson, Gerald Ratner, Carole Scott, Steven Stewart, Katrin Suesser and Mark Wenham who all enriched the book with their experience, wisdom and insight.

My sincere thanks to Sue Boxall and Louise Raisbeck who devoted many hours to reading my initial draft and provided invaluable feedback; the book is so much better as a consequence.

Special mention also goes to Gus Whitcomb who has been unfailingly generous with his time and expertise and was kind enough to write the Foreword. I only hope that the high standard he set is matched by the rest of the book.

Thank you to my exceptionally talented and supportive colleagues Sophie Hunt and Alex Johnson who took the strain while I locked myself away to write this tome, to Jenny Payne for her dedication as chief researcher and Catherine Timms for, as always, impeccable administrative support.

Thanks also to the Friday morning peer mentoring crew – Andrew Armitage, Sophie Milliken, Simon Shepard and Paul Turner – who cajoled, inspired and (occasionally) bullied me to get to the end of this book. I wouldn't have made it without you.

Finally, my heartfelt thanks to Tracy, James and Eleanor who have supported and encouraged me throughout this process and always believed I had a book in me, even when I sometimes didn't.

The Author

Jonathan Hemus is Managing Director of crisis management consultancy Insignia, and was previously Global Head of Crisis and Issues Management at international consultancy Porter Novelli.

He works with business leaders to ensure they have the capability and confidence to do and say the right things under the intense pressure of a crisis. During his twenty-five-year career he has advised clients including Anglo American, Cathay Pacific, Disney, DP World, the International Cricket Council, Lidl and Procter & Gamble.

Driven by a passion to prevent the needless harm caused by a mishandled crisis, he enables his clients to successfully prepare for and sometimes handle their worst nightmares, whether cyber-attack, catastrophic accidents, management misdeeds, product contamination or environmental incidents.

Jonathan is a regular media commentator on breaking crises for media, including the BBC, CNN, *Management Today*, *Sunday Times* and the *Wall Street Journal*, and is a visiting lecturer for Aston University Business School's MSc in Crisis and Disaster Management. He is also chair of the Advisory Board for Aston's Crisis Centre.

Outside of work, he enjoys a summer's day at the cricket, following his beloved Aston Villa and, as an antidote to stress caused by the latter, a brisk walk through Sutton Park (or alternatively a glass of Australian Shiraz).

To assess your crisis readiness, complete the Crisis Scorecard https://scorecard.insigniacomms.com /p/impact-scorecard or find Jonathan at:

✉ j.hemus@insigniacrisis.com
🌐 insigniacrisis.com, jonathanhemus.com
🐦 @jhemusinsignia
in https://www.linkedin.com/in/jonathanhemus/